The Truth and the Light
Jesus was a Servant and Prophet of God

By: Adebola Sanusi

Publisher's Name: Adebola Sanusi

ISBN: 978-1-962142-74-8

eBook ISBN - 978-1-962142-75-5

Table o f Contents

Preamble

In the name of Allah, Most Gracious, Most Merciful.

I give thanks to Almighty Allah, the Cherisher, Provider, Sustainer, Omnipotent, Omniscience and the Decider of all affairs. The only One Who deserves to be worshipped and who has no partner, no son, no beginning and no end.

I praise Him and glorify His name. I seek His assistance and guidance for giving me the thought of writing this book. I am asking Allah (SubHanahu Wa ta'ala) to shower His blessing upon the noble Prophet Muhammad (Peace be upon him) whom He sent as a savior for all mankind and Jinn. May Allah radiate His light upon the readers to know the truth and follow His path (amen).

I am going to make a quick reference to Hadith number #1 of the holy Prophet Muhammad (peace and blessing of Allah be upon him). He says, "Every act with intention." If your intention is to do things for the sake of Allah and His messenger, you will get your reward based on that. But if your intention is for the worldly thing, you will also get your reward.

Since the day I thought about writing this book, one sister, Alhaja R. Olayokun, sent me Sheik Muhammad Awal's video on my WhatsApp as if she had read my mind. This was the beginning of the inspiration. I was also talking with the late Alhaj Sheriff Adeleke (may Allah forgive his shortcomings and put him in paradise – ameen) one day after Jumat service, he too referred me to Sheik Yusuf Adepoju, and from there, most of the materials were just coming from different angles and I was also busy verifying the information.

This shows that when one has good intention, God will give direct and guide.I also give thanks to the following people who helped to edit this book such as Sheik Muhammad Salem,

Agwa, Sheik T. Idowu Bakare, and Dr. Imaddudin Hashmi. I thank those that I listened to their videos such as Sheik Muhammad Awal, Sheik Yusuf Adepoju, Late Sheik Ahmad Deeda, Ustaz Jamiu Adegunwa and Sheik Lukmon Adeyemo for their contributions and others that I don't know whom Allah used to send useful information.

I am using this opportunity to give special thanks and appreciation to Professor Yushau Sodiq for his tremendous contribution and assistance in the successful outcome of this book. May Almighty Allah increase his knowledge, long life and good health and reward all of them (Amen).

Quick Background of the Author

After elementary education, the author went to an Arabic and Islamic Training Center. He then proceeded to high school, where he studied Bible Knowledge and later went to college to major in Political Science,Philosophy and minor in International Relations. While in college, he studied Comparative Religion.*

---

* FOOTNOTES: Allah (God). SAW means – peace be upon him (PBUH). Shaitan- Satan, devil or Lucifer, or Iblis. (AS) Peace be upon him. Angels (Malaika)

Chapter 1

Introduction

In the name of God, the Beneficent, the Merciful. All praises are due to God, the Lord of all the worlds.

This work is an invitation to a healthy dialogue between Muslims and Christians in particular, and among all other traditions in general. It elaborates how Christians strive tirelessly to convert Muslims, by all means, and how Muslims respond to such unhealthy invitations because Nigerian Christians allege that Muslims have no knowledge of Jesus or Mary. The work explains the major differences between Islam and Christianity. It invites readers to contemplate the proofs presented by Islam and Christianity in ascertaining their claims to the truth and asks the readers to make their judgement thereof based on the quality of the evidence and on their common sense. My critique of Christianity regarding the lordship of Jesus (pbuh), as presented by the canonical Gospels and by St. Paul, is to give ample chance for concerned Christians to re-evaluate, re-read their claims with critical eyes, hoping that their convictions are based on the truth as espoused in the Bible, which they regard as the words of God. I substantiate whatever I present here, either on Christianity or Islam, with concrete evidence from the Bible or the Quran. I believe that both scriptures are revelations from God and hence urge each group to contemplate what the scripture asserts and abide by it. My conviction is that if each group allows what its scripture teaches, we'll be better off. I also appeal in this work to the development of mutual understanding among ourselves so that we can live together harmoniously without perceiving the other group as a lost sheep or looking to one another with contempt and disregard. God, the Creator of everything, loves us and thus sends to us different revelations to guide us to the right path so that we may enjoy a meaningful life. I pray that this work unites us and brings us together; after all, we are all humans and neighbors. We should live together harmoniously without harming one another.

I am prompted to write this book in view of hatred, disunity, injustice, oppression, unjust wars and the killings of the innocent perpetrated by the so-called "Religious people." Since most of the world population believes in one religion or another, religion is supposed to be a rope that unites the world but unfortunately, it has become a ticking time bomb that is now destroying world peace.

Another factor which motivates me in writing this book is the pressure I received from friends, coworkers and the preaching of some evangelical priests who try to condemn one religion over another. Religion is a delicate issue to dabble into. Quran chapter 2:256 says: "There shall be no compulsion in the religion." Also, Quran chapter 109:6: "To you be your way (religion), and to me mine"; that is practice any religion of your choice once the truth has come to you. Based on this view, I must give credit to the founding fathers who wrote the American Constitution for their vision and foresight of separating religion from state. This is to avoid religious wars that might engulf nations and push them into unnecessary destruction. Whatever your faith is, keep it to yourself and don't try to force or impress your religious views on others. And that has kept America safe since its inception.

But today, little by little, people are moving away and indirectly and publicly arguing that one religion is better than the other. I was watching Television one Sunday morning in 2007, when I heard the late Reverend Billy Graham, calling on Muslims to accept Jesus in their lives as that is the only way to salvation. I thought in my mind, what did this man know about Islam! Then at every corner of the subway, ferry or bus terminal, on the television and with friends, it is like a war of survival. Everyone is now preaching that accepting Jesus in one's life is the only way to heaven or paradise. This statement is totally incorrect and uncritical. I have friends who are pressuring me to convert to Christianity that I will be an asset to their religion and to my surprise; I have been receiving books from Christian folks on how some Muslims have embraced Jesus in their lives.

In the book titled *HEROES AND HERO WORSHIP*, by Thomas Carlyle alleging that Muhammad was a false prophet. He says:

> "A false man found a religion." Why, a false man cannot build a brick house! If he does not know and truly follow the Properties of mortar burnt clay and what else he works in, it is no house that he makes, but a rubbish-heap. It will not stand for twelve centuries, to lodge a hundred and eighty million; it will fall straightway" (article published in 1841).

This statement by Mr. Carlyle is a blasphemy and insult to our noble prophet Muhammed (peace be upon him). I wish Mr. Thomas Carlyle is alive today to come and see that the religion of Islam is not only in existence but it is the most fast-growing religion with a population of over one billion people.

In the later part of his life, when the truth about Islam cleared to him, he changed his mind and read later what he said about the Prophet and Islam.

Then I remember what Allah said about the Christians and Jews in the Holy Quran chapter 2 verses 111 and 135-136:

> 111 – And they say: "None shall enter paradise unless he be a Jew or Christian." Those are their (vain) desires. Say: "Produce your proof if you are truthful."

> 135 – They say: "Become Jews or Christians if ye

would be guided (to Salvation)." Say thou: "Nay! (I would rather) the Religion of Abraham, the True, and he joined not gods with Allah."

136 – Say ye: "We believe in Allah, and the revelation given to us, and to Abraham, Ismail, Isaac, Jacob, and the Tribes, and that given to Moses and Jesus, and that given to (all) Prophets from their Lord: we make no difference between one another of them: and we bow to Allah" (in Islam).

My colleagues at work who are Christians always come up with this conversation on how Islam cannot be a true religion. I tried to avoid it, but they kept coming. My partner is a member of Seventh Day Adventists, she is a very nice woman, she likes to learn or ask questions about Islam as I also asked questions about Christianity. I enjoyed my conversation with her; however, I disagree with most of her explanations peacefully without hurting her feelings. And when I ask questions that she cannot answer, she will find the answer from her Pastor. But I have one friend, who is like a brother and uncle to me, he is also a former coworker; whenever he finds a video of any Muslim convert, he will not hesitate to send it to me. And when I listen to the background of these converts, I can see that they are not practicing Muslims. One typical example, a woman claimed to have been born in Kenya in a family of practicing Muslims and she did not know who Prophet Muhammad was and had no knowledge of the Quran. This woman claimed that the religion of Islam is a violent religion. But when she came to America, she found that Jesus (PBUH) said in the Bible: "Talk to your enemy," and when she saw that, she converted to Christianity. After viewing the video, I called this uncle and said, "You just believed this woman's story, but her story did not add up to me"; he didn't like my answer. I told him, "With due respect, sir, please, I don't want to be engaged

4

in this type of uncritical conversation."

Two weeks later, another video from this uncle came again, where an artist— a musician in Nigeria—made a testimony in a church about how he was born Muslim and every year he would invite the alfas (Muslim scholars) to his house to pray for him and his family. And after they would have left, he would go and read the bible to sanctify their prayers. He said he went to hajj and every December 31st, if he doesn't go to church to pray, he will not have peace. He said, all his family -- his own wife and children, are Christians and he remains a Muslim, but now he cannot hide anymore and that is why he is coming out so he could declare openly that he is a new-born Christian. The whole church was rocked with "Praise the Lord." I texted this uncle to ask him what his point was here. First, many Nigerian Muslim families in the West are not practicing Islam but they are Muslims only by names. And when they have a newborn, they will call the Imam to do the naming ritual in Islamic way. The child will grow up with a Muslim name, no knowledge of Islam and will go to Christian school because of the few Islamic institutions that are available and maybe eventually become a Christian. Some of the musicians in Nigeria are illiterates but for the recording company to market their products, the first thing they will do is to send them to Mecca in Saudi Arabia to become Alhaj or Alhaja, they will now use this title to earn recognition in the society. However, the business promoters did not care about the artist's religion, only to make their own money out of them. This person has no Islamic background, and this is what this uncle used to call my attention to the fact that Islam is not the right religion but Christianity. He forgot that many Christians are converting to Islam in Nigeria as well as in America.

Another reason why some Muslims convert to Christianity is that they see Christian religion as a religion of convenience. It is a religion whereby anything and everything is acceptable and right to do if the pastor endorses it not the Bible.

Some of the inconveniences are due to the importance of cleanliness, because you don't have to clean with water for every use of the bathroom—urination or defecation. It is not compulsory to have a special bath like it is for Muslims whenever there's an intercourse with one's spouse before worshiping God. You don't have to pray five times daily. And more importantly, the Bible is written in the English language that is very easy for them to read. Another significant reason for their conversion is that they see Christianity as a quick way to make money (commercialization). One of the alleged miracles of Jesus is that wherever his picture is hung up, money will start to come into that place. If the church decides to raise a certain amount of money, if Jesus' photo is there, that amount will be raised. Quran surah Maryam chapter 19:31: "And He (God) hath made me blessed whosoever I be…." Many of these people are Muslims by names. Muslims are now pastors and reverends in many churches in Nigeria, including here in America. One of the quickest ways to become rich in Nigeria and Africa today is to build a church and maintain committed and loyal Christian members.

Furthermore, another simple trick the Christians use to convert Muslims, whether you are devoted or not, try to please you in any shape or form; including rendering financial assistance or accommodation if you are their guest. They applied this weapon as a means of enticement. They want to take you to the Church, and the moment you refuse, you have become their number one enemy. The next thing you will experience is that this entire accolade will seize, hostility will begin, and the next attitude is eviction from their homes. Their relationship with others is based on utility.

My dialogues with my Christian friends always happen because they always believe or insist that Jesus is the only way to salvation and paradise. And when I ask them if they have any knowledge about Islam or Quran, the answer is no. I told them that it is wrong of them to condemn one religion when they are totally ignorant of what another religion is all about. And for one to authoritatively and categorically say Jesus is the only way is totally wrong, because Jesus is not mentioned in the Bible as the only savior. In Matthew 5:17, Jesus said: "Think not that I am coming to destroy the law, or the prophets: I am not come to destroy, but to fulfil." This was the same message of Abraham, Noah, Solomon, Moses and Jesus (peace be upon them).

If you follow their messages revealed to them by God, you will enter the Kingdom of God.

I told my friends that being a Muslim, I studied Bible, Quran and did comparative religion. I can compare and I know the basic teaching of each religion in the world. I told them that we could not have a meaningful discussion when they had no idea of what the Quran says. And another area of our disagreement is the notion that Jesus is the son of God, the Holy Spirit and God Himself, when the Quran says he (Jesus) was the servant and messenger of God. In Quran Surah 19:30, as a day-old child, Jesus spoke in defense of his mother who was accused of immorality by saying: "I am indeed a servant of Allah: He had given me revelation and made me a prophet." Or when they say we all worship one God! I told them we Muslims recognize Jesus as a messenger of Allah but not God. And we worship Allah alone. John 17:3: "Now this life is eternal: that they may know you, the only true God, and Jesus Christ, whom you have sent."

According to Quran chapter 2:285 (Surah Al Baqarah):

> The Messenger believeth in what has been revealed to him from his Lord, as do the men of faith. Each one (of them) believeth in Allah, His angels, His books, and His messengers.
>
> "We make no distinction (they say) between one another of His messengers." And they say: "We hear, and we obey: (we seek) thy forgiveness, our Lord, and to Thee is the end of all journeys."

We Muslims strongly believe in Prophet Isa (Jesus-pbuh) and accord him great respect. In contrast, the Christians do not believe in Prophet Muhammed (Pbuh) and they despise him and call him bad names. When I ask them why, their answer is that Jesus is a living God who came in human flesh to sacrifice himself for the sins of human beings and that was why he died on the cross. The Christian definition of Jesus is very confusing and not only to me but to themselves. Sometimes Jesus is referred to as God, the Father, sometimes he is the son of God, and sometimes he is the Holy Spirit (Holy Trinity, 3 in 1 or 1 in 3).

I have a friend who is a barber, and nobody remembers his real name anymore because he renamed himself as "Omo Jesu," meaning the son of Jesus. He pressured me to come to Christianity that I must allow Jesus in my life. He tried to convince me to be a Christian claiming that I will be a good asset to them. I always laugh at him. He seems brainwashed, ignorant and misguided like others. He cannot quote a single ayah (verse) of the Holy Quran or quote a Hadith—from the sayings and deeds of the prophet Muhammed (saw). He didn't bother to learn anything about Islam except that Islam is not good for me

But recently, I finally found a Christian, Mr. Harrison Ogbolu, who believed in Prophet Muhammed (Pbuh) as a Messenger of God contrary to other Christians. This person is one of my colleagues at work who was recently transferred to my unit, and we were talking one day when he told me how he disagreed with Christians preaching against Muslims. I was surprised and asked him why. He now revealed to me that he was a Pastor before he left Nigeria, that he belonged to the Redeem Church of Christ and later joined the Pentecostal Church here in the United States. The reason for his switch was that he always challenged the Christians that Muslims believe in Jesus Christ, while the Christians don't believe in Prophet Muhammed. I asked him what their response was. He said they told him the Bible says Jesus Christ is the only way to heaven. Pastor Ogbolu said he asked the Christian folks, "Who wrote the Bible? Are they not human beings? Was the Bible written when Jesus was alive?" He challenged the collection of the Tithes and its distribution among the top members of the Church. Eventually, he was castigated as a rebel. He then left the Redeem Church. Pastor Ogbolu gave me permission to quote him in my book and he is ready to challenge any Christians on these issues according to his belief and understanding of the Bible.

I made my own personal research into the concept of Jesus as Holy Trinity (three in one).

An apology to those who may be angry at the revelation of the truth that I discovered, but at the end, you are entitled to form your own opinion or make your own judgment based on the facts presented to you and as you comprehend them.

This book attempts to set the record straight, free from misconceptions, misinterpretations and deceit.

I know the truth is bitter, but hold your breath and enjoy it. It is the truth that can make all of us safe and free.

Chapter 2

Who is Allah (God)

The definition of God according to the Bible:

Who is God?

The fact of God's existence is so conspicuous, both through creation and through man's conscience. The Bible calls the atheist a "fool" (Psalm 14:1). Interestingly, the Bible never attempts to prove the existence of God; rather, it assumes His existence from the very beginning (Genesis 1:1). What the Bible does is that it reveals the nature, character, and work of God.

Who is God? - The Definition

Thinking correctly about God is of utmost importance because a false idea about God is idolatry. In Psalm 50:21, God reproves the wicked man with this accusation: "You thought I was altogether like you." To start with, a good definition of God is "the Supreme Being; the Creator and Ruler of all that is; the Self-existent One who is perfect in power, goodness, and wisdom."

Who is God? - His Nature

We know certain things to be true of God for one reason: in His mercy He has condescended to reveal some of His qualities to us. God is spirit, by nature intangible (John 4:24). God is One, but He exists as three Persons—God the Father, God the Son, and God the

10

Holy Spirit (Matthew 3:16-17). God is infinite (1 Timothy 1:17), incomparable (2 Samuel 7:22), and unchanging (Malachi 3:6). God exists everywhere (Psalm 139:7-12), God knows everything (Psalm 147:5; Isaiah 40:28), and He has all power and authority (Ephesians 1; Revelation 19:6).

Who is God? - His Character

Here are some of God's characteristics as revealed in the Bible: God is just (Acts 17:31), loving (Ephesians 2:4-5), truthful (John 14:6), and holy (1 John 1:5). God shows compassion (2 Corinthians 1:3), mercy (Romans 9:15), and grace (Romans 5:17). God recognizes sin (Psalm 5:5) but also offers forgiveness (Psalm 130:4).

Who is God? - His Work

We cannot understand God apart from His works, because what God does flows from who He is. Here is an abbreviated list of God's works, past, present, and future: God created the world (Genesis 1:1; Isaiah 42:5); He actively sustains the world (Colossians 1:17); He is executing His eternal plan (Ephesians 1:11) which involves the redemption of man from the curse of sin and death (Galatians 3:13-14); He draws people to Christ (John 6:44); He disciplines His children (Hebrews 12:6); and He will judge the world (Revelation 20:11-15).

Who is God? - A Relationship with Him

In the Person of the Son, God became incarnate (John 1:14). The Son of God became the Son of Man and is therefore the "bridge" between God and man (John 14:6; 1 Timothy 2:5). It is only through the Son that we can have forgiveness of sins (Ephesians 1:7), reconciliation with God (John 15:15; Romans 5:10), and eternal salvation (2 Timothy 2:10). In Jesus Christ "all the fullness of the Deity lives in bodily form" (Colossians 2:9). So, to really know who God is, all we must do is look at the above attributes.

https://www.biblestudytools.com

Definition of God according to Torah.

According to the Torah, "God" is referred to as Yahweh (pronounced "Yah-weh"), represented by the Hebrew letters YHWH, which is considered the proper name of God in Judaism and is revealed to Moses in the book of Exodus; this name is often substituted with "Adonai" (Lord) due to its sacred nature and the tradition of not pronouncing it aloud.

Key points about God in the Torah:

Name:

The most common name for God in the Torah is "Yahweh" (YHWH), also called the TetragramMaton.

Meaning:

"Yahweh" is understood to mean "I Am Who I Am".

Pronunciation:

Due to its sanctity, Jews traditionally do not pronounce "Yahweh" aloud and instead use "Adonai" (Lord).

Relationship with the Israelites:

In the Torah, Yahweh is presented as the God of the Israelites, who chose them as his people and delivered them from slavery in Egypt.

Traditionally, Judaism holds that Yahweh is the god of Abraham, Isaac and Jacob, and the national god of the Israelites.

https://en.wikipedia.org

Who is God According to Islam?

God is Allah in Islam.
In the Quran, Allah is the name for the one God, who is described as the creator of the universe, the judge of humankind, and the sustainer of the world.

Attributes of Allah in Islam

Omnipotent: Allah has unlimited power

Omniscient: Allah has unlimited knowledge

All-merciful: Allah is infinitely merciful

Eternal: Allah has always existed and will always exist

Unique: Allah is one and indivisible

Allah's Relationships to humans

Allah revealed the Quran to the prophet Muhammad

Humans should submit to Allah's will

Allah will judge all humans on the Day of Judgment

Other descriptions of Allah in the Quran.

Allah is also known as the Lord of the Worlds

Allah is described as "Most Gracious, Most Merciful"

Allah is described as "the One and Only".

https://en.wikipedia.org,wiki,Allah

In Surah Yunus, Quran 10:3, Surah Al-A'raf, Quran 7: 54 and Surah Al- Hadid, Quran 57:4

The Quran states that Allah created the heavens and the earth, and everything between them in six days. Allah established Himself on the Throne. He knows what goes down into the earth and what comes out of it, and what descends from the above and what ascends to it. He is with you wherever you may be. Allah is watchful of all that humans do.

Quran 31:29-31 Surah Luqman

(31:29) Do you not see that Allah makes the night phase into the day and makes the day phase into the night and has subjected the sun and the moon to His will so that each of them is pursuing its course till an appointed time? (Do you not know that?) Allah is well aware of all that you do?

(31:30) that is because Allah ˹alone˺ is the Truth and what they invoke besides Him is falsehood, and ˹because˺ Allah ˹alone˺ is the Most High, All-Great.

(31: 31) Do you not see that the ships sail ˹smoothly˺ through the sea by the grace of Allah so that He may show you some of His signs? Surely in this are signs for whoever is steadfast, grateful.

Quran Relationship to the Bible

The Quran and the Bible describe God in similar ways, including viewing Allah as the Creator and Judge of the world. Both books also describe God as merciful and all-powerful.

According to the description of God by the three religions only the Bible described God as three in one. He exists as three Persons—God the Father, God the Son, and God the Holy Spirit. The Bible describes God as human-being, "So, to really know who God is, all we have to do is look at Jesus". This is a contradiction. God, the Almighty, was in existence before the birth of Jesus (pbuh) 2025 years ago. God is still alive after the death of Jesus or his crucifixion.

In the Quran Surah Al Maida, Quran 5: 72-77

72- Certainly, they disbelieve who say:

"Allah is Christ the son of Mary." But said the Jews.

"O Children of Israel! Worship Allah, my Lord and your Lord." Whoever joins other gods with Allah, Allah will forbid him The Garden, and the Fire will be his abode. There will be no helpers for the wrongdoers, and no one to assist them.

73- They disbelieve who say:

Allah is one of three (In a Trinity :) for there is No god except

One God. If they, the Christians, desist not from what they are saying (their word of blasphemy), verily a grievous chastisement will befall the disbelievers among them.

74- Why can't they turn not to Allah and seek His forgiveness?

For Allah is Oft-forgiving, Most Merciful.

75- Christ the son of Mary was no more than a Messenger; many were the Messengers that passed away before him. His mother was a woman of truth. They had both to eat their (daily) food. See how Allah doth make His signs clear to them; yet see in what ways they are deluded away from the truth!

76- Say: "Will ye worship, besides Allah, something which hath no power either to harm or benefit you?

But Allah, He is that heart and knoweth All things."

77- Say: "O people of the Book! (That is the Jews and Christians).

Exceed not in your religion the bounds (of what is proper). Trespassing beyond the truth, nor following the vain desires of people who went wrong in times gone by, who misled many, and strayed (themselves) from the even Way.

Note: in the scriptures, Torah and Quran, "God said no eyes can see Him, but He sees everything". But we saw Jesus who was born from a woman, circumcised, and breastfed, ate and slept as a characteristic of human being. How can human nature be attributable to God?

When in Luke 11: 27-28, a woman in the crowd exclaims that

the womb that bore Jesus (pbuh) and the breast that nursed him are blessed, but Jesus responds that true blessings belong to those who hear God's word and obey it.

According to Luke 2: 21: Jesus was circumcised and named on the eighth day after his birth, fulfilling the Jewish practice of circumcision and the name given by the angel before his conception. If these above attributes were attached to Jesus as a human being, how can the Christians call him God? Something must be wrong somewhere!

In Surah Al Mulk, Quran 67:1-3

1 - Blessed be He in whose hands are Dominion, and He over all things hath power;

2 - He Who created Death and Life, that He may try which of you is the best in action. He is the Exalted in Might, Oft-Forgiving;

3 - He who created the seven heavens one above another: No want of proportion wilt thou see in the Creation of The Most Gracious. So, turn thy vision again: Seest thou any flaw?

In Surah Al Fatiha, Quran 1: 1-7

1 - In the name of Allah, Most Gracious, Most Merciful.

2 - Praise be to Allah, The Cherisher and Sustainer of the Worlds:

3 - Most Gracious, Most Merciful;

4 - Master of the Day of Judgement.

5-Thee do we worship, and Thine aid we seek.

6-Show us the straight way,

7- The way of those on whom thou hast bestowed Thy Grace, Those whose (portion) is not wrath, and who go not astray (Ameen).

In Surah Yunus, Quran 10: 107

107-If Allah do touch thee with hurt/harm you, there is none can remove it but He:

If He does design some benefit for thee, there is none who can keep back His favor:

He causeth it to reach whomsoever of His servants He pleaseth. And He is the oft-Forgiving, Most Merciful.

In Surah Ar-Rahman, Quran 55: 26-27

26-All that is on earth will perish:

27- But will abide (forever) the Face of thy Lord, full of Majesty, Bounty and Honor.

This means that when the world comes to an end only Allah will remain.

In Surah Al Hadid, Quran 57: 1-3

1-Whatever is in the heavens and on earth, declares the Praises and Glory of Allah:

For He is the Exalted in Might, the Wise.

2- To Him belongs the dominion of the heavens and the earth:

It is He Who gives Life and Death; and He Has Power over all things.

3- He is the First and the Last, the Evident and the Hidden, and He has full knowledge of all things.

In Surah Al-Baqarah, Quran 2: 22 and 2:29

22- Allah Who made the earth your couch, and the heavens your canopy; and sent down rain from the heavens;

And brought forth therewith fruits for your sustenance; then set not up rivals unto Allah when ye know (the truth).

29- It is He Allah Who hath created for you all Things that are on earth; then He turned to the heaven and made them into seven firmaments.

And of all things He hath perfect knowledge.
Finally, the Surah Al-Ikhlas, Quran 112: 1-4 stated categorically that:

Say: He is Allah, the One;

Allah, the Eternal, Absolute;

He begetteth not, nor is He begotten;

And there is none like unto Him.

My fellow human-beings, we have seen the nature and characteristics of God. He created heaven and earth and all what is in there. He has no beginning and no end. He is not in Trinity as claimed by the Christians. Jesus (pbuh) who was born by a woman. Jesus has no power to do any of the attributes associated with Allah. Jesus ran away and hid when the Jews wanted to kill him. If Jesus were to be God as claimed by the Christians, he should have known the plot, blocked the plan and not run away.

How can the Christians worship a human-being like them and call him God?

Chapter 3

Religion

What is religion and how does it come into existence?

Religion has different shades of meanings and interpretations; some will be explained here.

Religion is a range of social-cultural systems, including designated behaviors and practices, morals, beliefs, worldviews, texts, sanctified places, prophecies, ethics, or organizations, that generally relate humanity to supernatural, transcendental, and spiritual elements.

https://en.wikipedia.org › wiki › Religion

1: a personal set or institutionalized system of religious attitudes, beliefs, and practices. 2. a (1): the service and worship of God or the supernatural.

https://www.merriam-webster.com › dictionary › religion

Religion is a belief in a god or gods and activities that relate to this belief, such as praying or worshipping in a building such as a church, temple or mosque and some worship in a shrine.

https://www.collinsdictionary.com/

Another definition of religion is human beings' relations to that which they regard as holy, sacred, absolute, spiritual, divine, or worthy of special reverence.

https://www.britannica.com/

In a nutshell, the concept of religion is more or less a social gathering of a group of people to worship the creator of the universe whom they believe control their destiny, who can provide for their sustenance, protect them from evils and whom they will be accountable to when they pass away.

The author wants to make a simple example of how to understand religion.

Religion is like politics where people or citizens must follow or obey the current administration. No one or some people will dare to say they will not follow the rules, decrees or legislation of the present regime but the old administration.

All the prophets of God came with a message from their Lord and whoever obeyed the prophets at their time will enter paradise. But between prophet Isa (the Jesus Christ) peace be upon him and the prophet Muhammad (peace be upon him) there was a gap of 570-600 years. Those who followed Jesus Christ after his departure from this world until the new prophet and messenger (prophet Muhammad (pbuh) came those people will enter paradise.

Since the prophet Muhammad (pbuh) was the last prophet, no one should follow any religion or doctrine but the doctrine and the message that the prophet Muhammad (pbuh) brought to this world. Prophet Muhammad's administration is still the current administration until the end of time.

The religion of Prophet Muhammad (pbuh) is Islam; Prophet Isa (Jesus Christ-pbuh) did not bring any other religion except the religion of Islam (submission to Allah) as you will see in another chapter. Jesus did not find or establish Christianity when he was alive. He was born a Jew and died as a Jew. Christianity as we know it today is alien to him. And the only religion practiced in heaven by the angels before Adam was created was Islam according to the Bible "Revelation 7:11).

The Almighty God is one and His religion is also one since the creation of Heaven and Earth.

According to the Bible in the Revelation 7:11-12

11- "And all the angels stood round about the throne, and about the elders and the four beasts, and fell before the throne, on their faces and worshipped God,

12- "Saying, Amen: Blessing, and glory, and wisdom, and thanksgiving, and honor, and power, and might, be unto our God forever and ever. Amen.

Please let us take note of the two verses seriously. If the angels were worshipping their Lord this way before Adam was created, and to be sincere to ourselves, what religion today worships like the angels?

The answer is Islam.

In the Quran, Surah Al-Imran, Chapter 3: 19 says:

19- "The religion before Allah is Islam (Submission to His Will): Nor did the People of the Book (that is Jews and Christians) dissent therefrom except through envy of each other, after knowledge had come to them. But if any deny the Signs of Allah, Allah is swift in calling (them) to account.

Since God is one, His religion must also be one as well.

Chapter 4

How do we have multiple religions

According to the Quran, Allah had created all things including Angels and Jinns before human- beings but wanted to put someone in charge. In Surah Al Baqarah, Quran 2: 30

30-"Behold, thy Lord said to the angels; "I will create a vicegerent on earth." (that is a representative to administer what Allah had created on earth), They said:

"Wilt Thou place therein one who will make mischief therein and shed blood?

Whilst we do celebrate Thy praises and glorify Thy holy (name)?"

He (Allah) said: "I know what ye know not".

Allah told the angels what He wanted to do, just for their information, and not that He was seeking permission from them.

That was the beginning of the creation of human-being, and he came into existence.

And Surah Al Araf, Quran 7: 11-25, gives us the root cause of human problems.

11- It is We Who created you and gave you shape:

Then We bade the angels prostrate to Adam, and they prostrated, not so Iblis; (Satan, devil, or Lucifer).

He refused to be of those who prostrated.

12- (Allah) said: "What prevented thee from prostrating when I commanded thee?

He (Satan) said: "I am better than he (Adam): Thou didst create me from fire, and him from clay".

13- (Allah) said: "Get thee down from it: It is not for thee to be arrogant here: get out, for thou art of the meanest (of creatures)."

14- He (Devil) said: "Give me respite till the day they are raised up."

15 - (Allah) said: Be thou among those who have respite."

16 - He (Satan) said: "Because thou have thrown me out (of the way), lo! I will lie in wait for them on Thy Straight Way:

17 - "Then will I assault them from before them and behind them, from their right and their left: nor will Thou find, in most of them, gratitude (for Thy mercies).

18 - (Allah) said: Get out from this, despised and expelled, if any of them follow thee, Hell will I fill with you all............ (Please complete the verses.

Because of this incident of disobedience of Satan and being kicked out from among the angels, he was determined to introduce many gods to human-being apart from the real God.

It was Devil, Satan or Lucifer that introduced so many religions to human-being to divert them from worshipping Allah, he misled people into worshipping the Sun, moon, water, snakes, monkeys, cattle, Iron, dragon to mention but few. Some people are also worshipping a fellow human being based on the miracles performed by the permission of their Lord who sent them.

Allah warns us in Surah Zukhruf, Quran 43: 62

62. "Let not Satan hinder or mislead you: for he is to you an enemy avowed."

In Torah, Nephi 28: 22

(For Satan) whispers in their ears and tells them there is no hell; and he says to them, "I am no devil, for there is none."

In Torah, Isiah 14: 15

"(That) you (O Lucifer), will be brought down to Hell, to the sides of the pit."

Today there are so many religions practiced but let us mention the most popular ones. They are Christianity, Islam, Buddhism, Hinduism; Judaism, Shintoism, Confucianism, Jainism, Bahai, Sikhism, Taoism, and Zoroastrianism, to mention but a few. However, among all these religions, only Islam is the religion of God, ordained for mankind and Jinn according to the holy Quran as we had mentioned earlier.

As part of Satan's power and influence, his avowed promise is to confuse the believers and divert their minds to worldly things especially when they are worshipping Allah. Therefore, he brainwashed the people to worship things that Allah created as gods. That is why we have many religions in the world today as people try to invent their own way of worship based on the doctrine of their founders. But on the day of judgement, this Satan will deny he ever forced them to do such.

The devil is taking revenge on the children of Adam because he was expelled and cursed because he refused to bow to Adam as instructed by Allah. Satan is irreconcilably jealous of the children of Adam.

It was Satan, who created enmity among people and instigated division among them to split them into sects for business purposes. For example, the devil brainwashed people to discard old Bible, and coerced them into believing that as followers of Jesus Christ, they are now newborn again. It was the same Satan (Lucifer) that encouraged people to change the Bible by having their own scriptures or doctrine and letting them see religion as a means of commercialization. At least there are about 153 or more different sects in the world today and all of them called themselves the followers of Jesus. The protestants that first broke away from the Catholic Church will never pray in the Catholic Church, the Baptist will never pray together with Jehovah witnesses because each has their own different Bibles and all of them proclaim they are the true followers of Jesus Christ to mention but a few. This statement is an eye-opener; it is something we see every day without embellishment. On a single street, you will see six or more separate Churches, but they will never worship together because their doctrines are different.

It is Lucifer who encourages Church leaders to seek extra power through Voodoos to do miracles like Jesus in order to get more members, whereas Jesus did not perform any miracles without the permission of his Lord.

Most of the injustices, oppressions, suppressions, embezzlements, rituals, human sacrifices, stealing and robbing, arrogance, cheating and causing chaos in the world today are the handiwork of Satan to make sure that he has large followers that will be with him in hellfire on the Day of judgement.

Chapter 5

The Creation of Human Beings

Allah, who is also known as "God," created all what is in heaven and earth. He created Angels and Jinns. He created all His creations in six days but never said He rested on the seventh day as some religious faiths have suggested. I don't know where human beings got the idea that God rests on Saturday or Sunday. Allah (God) stated in the holy Quran, Surah Al Rahman, Chapter 55:29:

"Of Him seeks (its need) every creature in heavens and on earths. Every day in (new) splendor doth He (shine)."

That is every creature depends on God, who works 24/7 without rest.

After all things had been created, God decided to create human beings as the custodian of His creations. God introduced democratic system by calling the angels and informing them about His plan to create human beings. Quran surah Al Baqarah - Chapter 2:30:

"Behold, thy Lord said to the Angels: 'I will create a vicegerent on earth.' They said: 'Wilt thou place therein one who will make mischief therein and shed blood? While we do celebrate Thy praises and glorify Thy Holy (Name)?' He (God) said, 'I know what ye know not.'"

The conversation of God with the Angels shows that jealousy did not start from human beings but jealousy and envy started with Angels, without knowing what type of human beings Allah (God) wanted to create, the Angels did not want rivals, I guess.

Allah gave Angels the structure of human beings and they

have no clue how it will turn out to be. God told angels to collect clay, mud or dust and mold it according to the structure or design. But the hadith of Prophet Muhammad (Pbuh) narrated by Ahmad, who said from Anas bin Malik, who stated that the Prophet said: "When Allah (God) created Adam, He left the structure there for as long as He wanted." Then Iblis, the Shaiton, devil, continued to circumambulate the structure, inspecting to see any default he can take advantage of. When the devil observed the hollow inside of the body, he found out that he (Adam) is weak, not strong enough to repel temptation. (Hadith Sahih Muslim # 2611)

Allah then breathed soul into Adam and impacted him with knowledge of His previous creations (Surah Al Baqarah, Quran, chapter 2:31). When God asked the angels to name certain things, the angels did not know them but when God asked Adam the names of His creations, Adam gave their names one after another. The Angels told Allah, "My Lord, we don't know anything except what you gave us knowledge about." Allah then commanded angels to bow to Adam, except Iblis, Shaiton (devil), who refused to bow to Adam. Shaiton answered! "You created Angels from Light; you created me from Fire, while You created Adam from Clay / Soil. I am better than him—Adam" (Quran 7:12).

God expelled the devil from among the angels. Shaitan (Satan, devil) told Allah, "Respite me till the day of judgment." Allah granted his request. But Shaitan said that "Every son of Adam, I am going to lie in wait for, on thy straight way. I will assault them both front and behind, mislead them, confuse them, deceive them and direct them away from your path." And Allah told Iblis (Shaitan) that "Those who are mine, you will not be able to confuse them because I will be sending messengers to them."

Surah Al Baqarah, Quran 2:38

38-We said: "Get ye down all from here; And if, as is sure, there comes to You Guidance from Me, whosoever follows My guidance, on them shall be no fear, nor shall they grieve.

After the creation of Adam and he was alone in paradise, Allah knew his life would be incomplete without a partner. He then created Hawa (Eve) from his ribs to be his wife and a companion in paradise. Allah gave them everything they could think of in paradise but warned them not to eat a fruit from a tree in paradise. But (Shaiton) convinced them (Eve and Adam) to eat from the forbidden tree. Their nakedness became open to them. God told Adam and Eve that for disobeying His order, He would expel them from paradise and send them to earth. Read more from Quran Surah Al A'raf, Chapter 7:11 – 25.

God told Adam and his wife that they shall eat from thy sweat and the consequence of their action is that they will die. Quran, Surah Ta Ha, Chapter 20:55: "From the (earth) did We create you, and into it shall We return you, and from it shall We bring you out once again." He also warned them about Shaitan, that he is their enemy, and they should not associate with him or be friendly with him.

Allah is a Merciful God. He doesn't want anyone to perish but to seek His forgiveness. In Surah Al-Baqarah, Quran 2:37, "Then learnt Adam from his Lord certain words and his Lord turned towards him; for He is Oft-Returning, Most Merciful. He told Adam that whenever you commit a sin seek forgiveness from your Lord. Adam did and Allah forgave him and his wife. Surah Al A'raf, Quran 7:23: "They said: Our Lord! We have wronged our own soul: If Thou forgive us not and bestow not upon us Thy Mercy, we shall certainly be lost."

CHAPTER 6

Building of a Nation

Quran Chapter 4:1, Surah Al Nisai; the Chapter of Women Allah stated that:

> "O mankind! Reverence your Guardian Lord, who created you from a single person, (Adam) created, of like nature, His mate, and from them twain scattered (like seeds) countless men and women—fear Allah, through Whom ye demand your mutual (rights), and (reverence) the wombs (that bore you): for Allah ever watches over you."

The 8.062 billion people in the world today came from these two people, Adam and Eve.

In Quran, Surah Al Hujurat, Chapter 49:13:

> Allah said: "O mankind! We created you from a single (pair) of male and female, and made you into nations and tribes, that ye may know each other (not that ye may despise each other). Verily the most honored of you in the sight of Allah is (he who is) the most righteous of you. And Allah has full knowledge and is well acquainted (with all things)."

God created us to love one another, to cater for each other, but we have allowed Satan to divide us and create enmity among us. The population of the world is not just multiplying by Allah asking the angels to collect clay, dust or mud as He did with Adam. He put reproductive elements in the human body, whereby whenever male and female mate by having sexual intercourse, the male's sperm strikes the egg in the female ovary with the power of God to: Be and it be.

The reproductive process begins, and the female becomes pregnant. During pregnancy, the development of human beings from fertilized eggs into blood clot into different types of human organs starts to show until formation of a complete human being, and then Allah will breathe soul into it. As the son of Adam, before human beings are born into this world, each individual has a covenant with Allah known as Fitrah.

Chapter 7

Covenant with Allah (God)

Every child born or unborn as the son of Adam made covenant with God that he/she will not worship any other God than Allah; that he/she will submit to the will of Almighty God, and that Islam will be his/her religion (http://soulreadingzone.com/tag/covenant-with-god).

Allah reminded us in the Holy Quran, surah Al A'raf, chapter 7 verse 172:

> "When thy Lord drew forth from the children of Adam from their loins—their descendants, and made them testify concerning themselves, (saying): 'Am I not your Lord (who cherishes and sustains you)?' They said: 'Yea! We testify!' (This I, lest ye should say on the Day of Judgment.) 'Of this we were never mindful."

Prophet Muhammad (Pbuh) explained further in his hadith: Abu Huraira reported Allah's messenger (Pbuh) as saying: "No child born but upon Fitra naturally(as a Muslim). It is his/her parents who make him/her a Jew or a Christian or Polytheist. (Hadith Sahih Muslim # 2658e – The Book of destiny).

In Quran 76 ayat 1-3:

> "There surely came over man a period when he was a thing not worth mentioning. Surely, we created man from

35

a small life—germ uniting (itself): We mean to try him,
so we have made him hearing and seeing. Surely, we have
shown him the way: he may be thankful or unthankful."

The above verse asserts that human beings have free will to choose what they want.

Based on this FREE Will, if anyone embraces another religion other than Islam, he will be responsible for his /her choice.

To keep up with this covenant, God continues to send prophets after prophets to remind human beings of their covenant when they were created, which they have forgotten due to pursuit of worldly things. The job of the prophets is to deliver the message of Allah that He alone is to be worshipped and not to associate a partner with Him. He encourages us to give alms/charity to the needy. God commands us to do good and be righteous. Whoever follows this message will enter paradise. Whoever disobeys the message will be punished by Allah if he /she does not repent. This is the same message delivered by Adam and other Prophets down to Prophet Muhammad (peace be upon them). No difference in their divine messages.

Chapter 8

Characteristics of the Prophets

According to the hadith in Musnad Imam Ahmad, narrated by Abu Umanah Al-Bahili relating a conversation Abu Dhar had with the Messenger of Allah (pbuh): he said: "O Messenger of Allah, how many Prophets were there?" He said: "One hundred and twenty-four thousand (124,000) Hadith in Mishkalul Masabih Vol 3, # 5737, from which three hundred fifteen (315) were Jamma ghafeera." Quran mentions 25 of them and five of these are in the highest positions (Ulul-Al-Azm - Determined messengers, http://islam.stackexchange.com/questions).

God sent some of them to their wives alone or to their children alone, while some were sent to their tribes, including Moses and Isa (Jesus: Peace be upon them). Both are sent specifically to the Bani – Israel (the Israelites). Jesus said in the Bible in Matthew 15:22-24: "I am not sent but unto the lost sheep of the house of Israel." Read more, Matthew 10:5-6, where Jesus instructed his disciples, "These twelve Jesus sent forth, and commanded them, saying, 'Go not into the way of the Gentiles, and into any city of the Samaritans enter ye not: But go rather to the lost sheep of the house of Israel." Matthew 19:28: "And Jesus (Pbuh) said unto them, 'Verily I say unto you, That ye which have followed me, in the regeneration, when the Son of man shall sit in the throne of his glory, ye also shall sit upon twelves' thrones, judging the twelve tribes of Israel." Quran 3:49, God appointed Jesus an apostle to the children of Israel. Quran 43:59 says: "He Jesus was no more than a servant: We granted our favor to him, and made him an example to the children of Israel." *It was only Prophet*

Muhammad (Pubh) that God sent to the whole of mankind and Jinns. Quran surah Al Anbiya (21:107): "We sent thee not, but as a mercy for all creatures."

Surah Yunus (Quran 10:47): To every people (nation) was sent a Messenger, Surah Saba (Quran 34:28):

> "We have not sent thee but as a <u>universal Messenger.</u>
> To men giving them glad tidings and warning them against sin, but most men understand not."

This shows that only Prophet Muhammad (Peace be upon him) was sent to the whole world.

All these prophets delivered the same message about the oneness of Allah (God). As for some Prophets, God gave them their respective scripture while the majority of them were just chosen by God. All or some of the prophets, Allah gave signs that make them different from ordinary human beings. God spoke to some of them directly such as Prophet Musa (Moses); to some others, angels were sent. God gave some of them power to perform miracles, some of them Allah endowed with wisdom to judge between people such as Prophet David (Daud) and Suleiman (Solomon).

MAN MADE DISTORTIONS:

I am going to give the proof from the Holy Quran only because the Bible and the Torah had distorted the account and accuracy of their stories, making them no longer tenable or trustworthy. The Bible was not written during the life of Jesus (Pbuh) and as such he was not alive to corroborate and proofread the story. The Christians have attached or ascribed unfounded embellishments/additions to their stories. Based on this distortion and falsification of their history, Allah said in the Holy Quran chapter 2:79:

"Then woe to those who write the Book with their own hands, and they say: 'This is from Allah,' to traffic with it for a miserable price! – Woe to them for what their hands do write, and for the gain they make thereby" (Surat Al-Baqarah, Ayah, 79).

This is the revelation by God, and no man has the right to change it or rewrite it; it must be left the way it was revealed. If you like it, follow it and if you don't like it leave it the way it was revealed without tampering with it to suit your purpose. But today, the Bible has so many versions. The Christians assembled their clergy to review the law of God by saying this is modern life and some of the laws are outdated, having been enacted in the medieval era, and not relevant to the present-day world. The Gospel of Thomas and Barnabas are no longer part of the Bible, they have been removed. And most Bibles do not have those verses anymore such as Mathew 17:21, Matthew 18:11, John 5:4, John 23: 14, Mark 7:16, 11:26, 15:28, Luke 17:36 and Roman 16:34 have been removed. Then you ask a question: Who has that power or audacity or authority to delete those verses and rewrite the words of God? They forgot that, the God of yesterday, is the God of today and the God of tomorrow. Where is the original Bible today?

Chapter 9

The Story of Mariam (Mary, Jesus' Mother, and the Birth of Jesus)

The Holy Quran gives more details about Maryam (Mary) and Isa (Jesus) than what is in the Bible; Q3:33-51, and Q19:16-37. Even Allah honored her (Maryam) by revealing a whole chapter (Chapter 19) in her name— Surah Maryam. This chapter, together with Chapter 3, gives a comprehensive narration of Mary's life with that of her son, Jesus (Pbuh).

Surah Al-Imran, Q3: 33-51:

33 – "Allah did choose Adam and Noah, the family of Abraham, and the family of 'Imran above all people.

34 – "Offspring, one of the other; and Allah heareth and knoweth all things.

35 – "Behold! A woman of Imran said: 'O my Lord! I do dedicate unto Thee what is in my womb for thy special service: so, accept this of me. For Thou hearest and knowest all things.'

36 – "When she was delivered, she said: 'O my Lord! Behold! I am delivered of a female child!' and Allah know best what she brought forth— 'and no wise is the male like the female. I have named her Mary, and I commanded her and her offspring to thy protection from the Evil one, the rejected.'

37 – "Right graciously did her Lord accept her: He made her grow in purity and beauty; to the care of Zakariya who was her custodian Every time that he entered (her) chamber to see her, he found her supplied with sustenance. He said: 'O Mary! Where (come) this to you?' She said: 'From Allah: for Allah provides sustenance to whom He pleases, without measure.'

38 – "There Zakariya prayed to his Lord, saying: 'O my Lord! Grant unto me from Thee a progeny that is pure: for Thou art He that heareth prayer!'

39 – "While he was standing in prayer in the chamber, the angels called unto him: 'Allah doth give the glad tidings of Yahya, witnessing the truth of a word from Allah, and (be besides) noble, chaste, and a prophet of the (goodly) company of the righteous.'

40 – "He said: 'Oh my Lord! How shall I have a son, seeing as I am very old, and my wife is barren?' 'Thus,' was the answer, ' Doth Allah accomplish what He willeth.'

41 – "He said: 'O my Lord! Give me a sign!' 'The Sign,' was the answer, shall be that thou shall speak to no man for three days but with signals. Then celebrate the praises of thy Lord again and again, and glorify Him in the evening and in the morning.'

42 – "Behold! The angels said: 'O Mary! Allah hath chosen thee and purified thee—chosen thee above the women of all nations.'

43 – "O Mary! Worship thy Lord devoutly: prostrate thyself and bow down (in prayer) with those who bow down.'

Let us take a note here, Allah did not instruct Mary to dance, sing or clap in worshipping Him but to bow and prostrate as the Muslims do which shows that Islam had been in existence before prophet Muhammad (pbuh) came.

44 – "This is the part of the tidings of the things unseen, which we reveal unto thee (O Prophet!) by inspiration. Thou wast not with them when they cast lots with arrows, as to which of them should be charged with the care of Mary: Nor was thou with them when they disputed (the point).'

45 – "Behold! The angels said: 'O Mary! Allah giveth the glad tidings of a word from Him: his name will be Christ Jesus. The son of Mary, held in honor in this world and the hereafter and of (the company of) those nearest to Allah.'

46 – "He shall speak to the people in cradle and in maturity. And he shall be (of the company) of the righteous.'

47 – *"She said: 'O my Lord! How shall I have a son when no man hath touched me?' He said: 'Even so: Allah created what he will: when he hath decreed a plan, He but said to it, Be! And it is!'*

48 – "And Allah will teach him the Book and Wisdom, the Law and the Gospel.

49 – "And (appoint him) a messenger to the <u>Children of Israel</u>, (with this message): 'I have come to you, with a sign from your Lord, in that I make for you out of clay, as it were, the figure of a bird, and breathe into it, and it becomes a bird by Allah's leave; and I declare you what ye eat, and what ye store in your houses. Surely therein is a sign for you if ye did believe.'

50 – "(I have come to you), to attest the Law which was before me. And to make lawful to you part of what was (before) forbidden to you; I have come to you with a sign from your Lord. So, fear Allah and obey me.'

51 – "It is Allah, who is my Lord, and your Lord then worship Him. This is a way that is straight."

Chapter   10

The Birth of Jesus (Isa)

Surah Maryam, Quran 19, Ayah 16-37:

The birth of Prophet Isa (Jesus - Pbuh) who was born, Yeshua or Yahushua is the original name as stated in Hebrew Biblical texts. Jesus is a name constructed by man through many versions of transliteration, from Hebrew to Greek, from Greek to Latin, from Latin to English. But who is Jesus? Another dispute on Jesus Christ revolves around the time and the circumstances of his birth. There is no biblical evidence suggesting an accurate date of his birth, even a mention of celebration commemorating the day of his birth. The first recorded date of Christmas was not until 336 A.D., during the time of the first Roman Christian Emperor Constantine. It was officially declared by Pope Julius 1 that December 25th would be the day of celebration of Jesus' birth.

I asked a friend of mine what she did for Christmas that year being a Christian woman. She said that she did not celebrate Christmas because neither she nor anyone else knows when Jesus' actual birth is.

According to the Holy Quran, when Mary was pregnant, she had been away from her kin for some time. But when she came back to the town and people saw her with her baby in her arms and never heard that she was married to a man, people began to wonder. Q19:16-36:

16 – "Relate in the Book (the story of) Mary, when she withdrew from her family to a place in the East.

17 – "She placed a screen (to screen herself) from them; then We sent to her Our angel, and he appeared before her as a man in all respects.

18 – "She said: 'I seek refuge from thee to (Allah) Most Gracious: (come not near) if thou dost fear Allah.'

19 – "He said: 'Nay, I am only a messenger from thy Lord, (to announce) to thee the gift of a holy son.'

20 – "She said: 'How shall I have a son, seeing that no man has touched me, and I am not unchaste?'

21 – "He said: "So (it will be): thy Lord saith, "That is easy for Me: and (We wish) to appoint him as a Sign unto men and a Mercy from Us": it is a matter (So) decreed.'

22 – "So she conceived him, and she retired with him to a remote place.

23 – "And the pains of childbirth drove her to the trunk of a palm tree:

She cried (in her anguish): 'Ah! Would that I had died before this! Would that have been a thing forgotten and out of sight!'

24 – "But (a voice) cried to her from beneath the (palm tree): 'Grieve not! For thy Lord hath provided a rivulet beneath thee;

25 – "And shake towards thyself the trunk of the palm tree; it will let fresh ripe dates fall upon thee.

26 - "So eat and drink and cool (thine) eyes. And if thou dost see any man say, 'I have vowed a fast to (Allah) Most Gracious, and this day will *enter into no talk with any human being.'*

27 – "At length she brought the (babe) to her people, carrying him (in her arms).

They said: 'O Mary! Truly an amazing thing hast thou brought!'

28 – "O sister of Aaron! Thy father was not a man of evil, nor thy mother a woman unchaste!"

29 – "But she pointed to the babe, they said: 'How can we talk to one who is a child in the cradle?'

30 – "He (Jesus-Pbuh) said: 'I am indeed a servant of Allah: He hath given me revelation and made me a prophet.'

31 – "And He hath made me blessed where so ever I be, and hath enjoined on me prayer and charity as I live.

32 – "(He) hath made me kind to my mother, and not over bearing or miserable.

33 – "So peace is on me the day I was born, the day that I die, and the Day that I shall be raised up to life (again)!

34 – "Such (was) Jesus the son of Mary: (It is) a statement of truth, about which they (vainly) dispute.

35 – "It is not befitting to (the majesty of) Allah that he should beget a son. Glory be to Him? When He determines a matter, He only says to it, 'Be, and it is.'

36 – "Verily Allah is my Lord and your Lord: He therefore serves ye: this is a way that is straight."

Summary

The Birth of Jesus is clear and simple: Allah (God) has power to do and create whatever He likes, the way He wants and at the time He chooses. To suggest then that Jesus is the son of God, the Holy Ghost and God Himself, is ridiculous and untrue. God further says in Chapter 3 of the Holy Quran:

59 – "Surely the likeness of Isa (Jesus) is with Allah as the likeness of Adam; He created him from dust, then said to him, Be, and he was.

Let us quickly look at Hawa (Eve), the wife of Adam, who Allah created from the rib of Adam, does she have a mother? No. Allah has the power to create anything He wants.

60 – "The truth (comes) from your Lord alone; so be not of those who doubt."

This is a day-old child defending his mother. And this is the first miracle performed by Jesus. You don't see this story in the Bible. To all Christians, the first miracle of Jesus is the turning of water into wine.

As said in the characteristics of prophets, Allah gave Moses the staff, which he used to command at will. This was his own power of miracle. He used this power to prove to Pharaoh that he was not the god as he claimed to be to the people, but to surrender to the will of one Almighty God. It was this miraculous staff that swallowed up all the materials produced by Pharaoh's magicians. It was this same staff that (prophet Moses-pbuh) used to divide the Red Sea, with the leave of Allah, and to save the children of Israel from Pharaoh. Despite all what Moses (Pbuh) did to save the Bani – Israel (Israelites) from the hands of pharaoh in Egypt, and took them to the Promised Land, the Jews did not believe in him and his message. They waged relentless wars against him and his followers.

Read more about the miracle of Moses to swallow the materials of Pharaoh's magicians from the Holy Quran, Surah Al Araf, chapter 7, verses 104-129 and in the Bible Exodus 7: 8-13.

Later, Allah sent another prophet to Bani – Israel (Israelites) in the name of Jesus the son of Mary and made his birth miraculous, hoping that with all the powers of his miracles that God gave him, he would be able to convince and with the people of his time to his message. Alas! The Jews did not want to believe him either.

Jesus was not sent to the whole of mankind, but to the Israelites alone as indicated in the Holy Quran, Chapter 3:49: "And appoint him—Jesus a messenger to the Children of Israel." Jesus said he was sent to the lost sheep of Israel (Matthew 15:24).

The question we ask our Christian friends is: Was Jesus Christ really born on December 25th? If he was not born on that day, why was he celebrated on that day?

Another question is: December 25th is the origin of Christmas, isn't it the tradition of the pagan holiday celebration of worshiping sun and moon gods? Why would the pagan holiday be adopted to be the birth of Jesus celebration?

CHAPTER 11

The Children of God in the Bible

The Christians believe that Jesus Christ (Pbuh) was the only son of God, whom God sent to sacrifice for the sins of the world. In the Bible according to Mark 1: 10-11, during the baptism of Jesus (pbuh) by John, the Baptist.

10 - "And straightway coming up out of the water, he saw the heavens opened and the Spirit like dove descending upon him:

11 - And there came a voice from heaven, saying, "Thou art my beloved Son, in whom I am well pleased."

If the Bible proclaimed that Jesus was the only beloved son of God, we believe this is metaphorically used. Jesus is not a biological son of God as there are many persons whom God called his sons. Let us look at the other sons of God mentioned in the Bible before Jesus was born.

In Psalm 89: 27, the Bible said that King David was the first son of God.

" Also I will make him my first born, Higher than the king of the earth. 2 Samuel 7:14 and 1 Chronicle 17:13 also confirm David was the first son of God.

In Isiah 43:6 and Hosea 1: 10 says: The Israelites were called the children of God.

1:10 " Yet the number of the children of Israel shall be as the sand of the sea, which cannot be measured nor numbered; and it shall come to pass, that in the place where it was said unto them, ye are not my people, there it shall be said unto them, ye are the sons of the living God."

In Luke 3:38, Adam was called the son of God

In Job 1:6, 2:1 and 38:7, Angels were called the sons of God.

In Exodus 4: 22, God told prophet Moses to tell Pharaoh, that Israel is my son.

"And thou shall say unto Pharaoh, Thus saith the Lord, Israel is my son, even my first born."

In 1 Chronicle 22: 9-10, Solomon was referred to as the son of God.

With all these children of God mentioned above, are they not confusing and misleading? With the above, it seems that God, the father, had many sons. Thus, how could the Bible now lay emphasis on Jesus Christ as the only son of God, what happened to the sons of God before Jesus was born?

Let us look at another area of controversy in the Bible.

In John 1.1, The Word became Flesh.

In the beginning was the Word, and the Word was with God, and the Word was God. Meaning that Jesus Christ existed with God and was God.

In Genesis 1.1, The Creation.

In the beginning God created heaven and the earth, meaning it was Jesus who created the universe. If Jesus was not the one who created heaven and earth (in the beginning) who created them? Muslims believe that the creator of the universe is Almighty God, who was there yesterday, He is there today. He will be there tomorrow.

In the same Bible, Melchizedek said, "he is indeed like Jesus without beginning or end and offers a sacrifice of bread and wine."

Hebrews 7:3, says that Melchizedek was "without father or mother without descent, having neither beginning of days, nor end of life, but made like unto the son of God; abideth a priest continually."

50

If we look critically into the composition of these important figures in the Bible, we can recognize some contradictions and inaccuracies. Jesus Christ has a mother but no father. Melchizedek has neither father nor mother and both were called the son of God. And both were in existence before the creation of heaven and earth. If Jesus were called God or son of God who came in the flesh, then who was Melchizedek?

How many Gods do we have and how many sons of God, does God have? Who is God among them?

It was because of the misleading information and contradictory statements by the Christian leaders that prevented the truth from prevailing. Many of these leaders know the truth but preach otherwise because of the material benefits they enjoyed through their members. These manipulation and indulgences are not new in the history of Christianity. Indeed, the Almighty Allah (God) due to His love for humanity sent Prophet Muhammad (Pbuh) to the world to correct and straighten all these controversies with the last revelation from Him, the Holy Quran, the guide for humankind and Jinn.

In Surah Maryam, Quran 19: 88-92, God affirms:

88 - They say: "The Most Gracious has taken a son! (that is, Christians alleged that God has taken a son)

89 - Indeed ye have put forth a thing most monstrous!

90 - At it (with this allegation that God has a son) the skies are about to burst, the earth to split asunder, and the mountains to fall down in utter ruin,

91 - That they attribute a son to The Most Gracious.

92 - For it is not consonant with the majesty of the Most Gracious that He should beget a son.

Also in Surah Al- An'Am Quran 6: 101

101- (God) the Wonderful Originator of the heavens
and earth:

How can He have a son when He hath no consort?
He created all things, and He hath full knowledge of all things.
Undoubtedly this is a clear statement from the Almighty Allah
(the One God) who has no partner or son.

It was an abomination and uncritical statement for Christians
to attribute a child or children to Allah (God).

May God guide us all to the right path and enable us to recognize
the truth all the times wherever it lies. Ameen.

Chapter 12

The Miracles of Jesus by the Leave of Almighty Allah

The Christians believe that the miracles performed by Prophet Isa (Jesus- Pbuh) the son of Mary have turned him or qualified him to be God as they claim. And they also misrepresent or misidentify his miraculous powers. If you ask the Christians, what was the first miracle performed by Jesus, the answer is always that he changed water into wine! Whereas the Holy Quran tells us in Chapter 19:27-36 as previously mentioned above regarding the conversation that transpired between Maryam, Isa and their people. But you will never find this revelation in the Bible. This was a day-old child defending his mother from accusation of immorality!

The Christians have committed great sins and continue to commit greater sins toward God the (Creator) by attributing this power of miracles solely to Jesus, when in fact Jesus himself attested to this power as being with the permission of Allah. In John 5:30, Jesus said: "I can of my own self do nothing: as I hear, I judge and my judgment is just; because I seek not my own will, but the will of the father which hath sent me."

Jesus was never proud of or boastful about his power of miracles to his followers, even when he raised Lazarus from the dead! When Martha, the sister of Lazarus, told Jesus about her brother's death, and they were on their way to the tomb where Lazarus was laid down, Jesus was communicating with God. The evidence for this is in the Bible, John 11:38–44.

38 – "Jesus therefore again groaning in himself cometh to the grave. It was a cave, and a stone lay upon it.

39 – "Jesus said, take ye away the stone, Martha, the sister of him that was dead, said unto him, Lord, by this time he stinks: for he had been dead four days.

40 – "Jesus saith unto her, said I not unto thee, that, if thou wouldest believe, thou shouldest see the glory of God?

41 – "Then they took away the stone from the place where the dead was laid. And Jesus (lifted his eyes, and said, Father; I thank thee that thou have heard me).

42 – "And I knew that thou hearest me always: but because of the people which stand by I said it, that they may believe that thou have sent me.

43 – "And when he had spoken, he cried with a loud voice, Lazarus, come forth.

44 – "And he that was dead came forth, bound hand and foot with grave clothes: and his face was bound about with a napkin. Jesus saith unto them, loose him, and let him go."

Here you can see that Jesus was crying and communicating with God to have power to raise Lazarus from the dead because only God alone can do that. But when he got assurance from God, he told the people to open the gate to where Lazarus was laid and woke him up from the dead. Not only that, but God also gave Jesus powers to open the eyes of the blind, to cure some diseases that were afflicting human beings with no cure at that time, just for the people of Israel to believe in him as a messenger of God. But instead, his followers believe that he is God himself.

The Almighty Allah says in Surah Al Maida, Quran (5:110, and 113-118):

110 – "Then will Allah say: 'O Jesus the son of Mary!

Recount My favor to thee and to thy mother. Behold! I strengthened thee with the Holy Spirit, so that Thou didst speak to the people in cradle and in maturity. Behold! I taught thee the Book and Wisdom, the Law and the Gospel. And behold! Thou makest out of clay, as it were, the figure of a bird by My leave, and thou breathest into it, and it becometh a bird by My leave, and thou healest those born blind, and lepers, by My leave. And behold! Thou bringest forth the dead by My leave.

And behold! I did restrain the children of Israel from (violence to) thee when thou didst show them the clear signs and the unbelievers among them said: "This is nothing but evident magic."

Evidence of this divine intervention in Jesus' miracles is also mentioned in John 5:19 and John 5:30:

But let us read the below statement from the holy Quran (5:113-118).

113 – "They said: 'We only wish to eat thereof and satisfy our hearts, and to know that thou hast indeed told us the truth; and that we ourselves may be witness to the miracle.'

114 - "Said Jesus the son of Mary: 'O Allah our Lord! Send us from heaven a table set (with viands), that there may be for us for the first and last of us a solemn festival and a sign from Thee; and provide for our sustenance, for thou art the best sustainer (of our needs).'

115 – "Allah said: 'I will send it down unto you; but if any of you after that resist faith, I will punish him with a penalty such as I have not inflicted on anyone among the peoples.'

116 – "And behold! Allah will say: 'O Jesus the son of Mary! Didst thou say unto men, "worship me and my mother as gods in derogation of Allah?" He will say: "Glory to Thee!" Never could I say what I had no right (to say). Had I said such a thing, Thou wouldst indeed have known it. Thou knowest what is in my heart, though I know not what is in Thine. For Thou knowest in full all that is hidden.'

117 – "Never said I to them aught except what thou didst command me to say, to wit, "Worship Allah, my Lord and your Lord: and I was a witness over them whilst I dwelt amongst them; when thou didst take me up thou wast the watcher over them, and Thou art a witness to all things."

118 – "If Thou dost punish them, they are thy servants: If thou dost forgive them, thou art the Exalted in power, the Wise." This was the response Jesus gave to Allah.

Evidence of this divine intervention in Jesus' miracles is also mentioned in John 5:30

As said in the previous chapter, God gave the prophets some extraordinary powers to prove to their respective nations that they were not just ordinary people like them to deliver the message of God. But because of these powers, the Jews and Christians have gone far in their interpretation of these powers. The Jews called

Uzair the son of God, while the Christians called Jesus, the son of Mary the son of God, or God himself. And Allah is unsatisfied with both faiths because of this stupid and blasphemous attribute attached to these two prophets. God has said that the creation of Jesus is like the creation of Adam. What is not clear about this if they are sincere in their faith? How dare someone say God has a son or a child. Who is God's wife? (Some said Mary).

Allah said in the Surah Al Ikhlas, Quran 112:1-4:

In the name of Allah, Most Gracious, Most Merciful.

Allah commanded the Holy Prophet Muhammad (saw) to tell the whole world including the Jinns that,

1 – Say: He is Allah – God; the one and only.

2 – Allah, the External, Absolute;

3 – He begetteth not, nor is He begotten;

4 – And there is none like unto Him.

In Quran chapter 6:101, Allah says,

"To Him is due the primal origin of the heavens and earth: how can He have a son when He hath no consort? He created all things, and He hath full knowledge of all things."

Even Jesus himself said: No one is "God" including Jesus. Only GOD is" God" (Luke 18:19).

Allah (Subhanahu Wa Ta'ala), vehemently repeated in the following chapters in the Holy Quran that He has no son.

Chapters 2:116 "They say: "Allah hath begotten a son:" Glory be to Him.-Nay, to Him belongs all that is in the heavens and on earth: everything renders worship to Him, Quran 9:30, 10:68 and 19:35

Why then do Jews and Christians ascribe sons to Almighty Allah?!

When Allah said the creation of Prophet Isa (Jesus) "Alaehi Salam, is like the creation of Adam. And when Allah wills something, He will just say to that thing: 'Be and it will be."

The assertion that Allah has a child has put doubt in the faith of the Jews and Christians and has reduced them in their faith to the category of pagans/polytheists.

Surah Al Tawbah, Quran 9:30-31:

30 – The Jews called "Uzair a son of God and the Christians call Christ the son of God." That is a saying from their mouth; (In this) they imitate what the unbelievers of old used to say, Allah's curse be on them: how they are deluded away from the truth!

31 – They take their priests and their anchorites to be their lords in derogation of Allah, and (they take as their Lord) Christ, the son of Mary; yet they were commanded to worship but one God: There is no god but He. Praise and glory to Him: (Far is He) from having the partners they associate (with Him).

If the followers of these two faiths have tried to recognize the Holy Prophet Muhammad (Pbuh) as a messenger of Allah, read the Holy Quran and believed in this overwhelming clear evidence that Allah rejects the claim of having a child, they could have challenged their own scriptures and those who have manufactured these bogus lies. But unfortunately, they didn't because they too benefit and profit from concealing the truth.

Before the birth of Jesus Christ, Allah (Subhanahu Wa Ta'ala) had given power of miracles to some prophets such as Prophets Ibrahim (Abraham), Sulaiman (Solomon), David and Idris (Enoch) to mention but a few.

Prophet Ibrahim (Abraham), when he asked Allah to convince him of the resurrection of the dead. Allah experimented on him by asking Ibrahim to take four different birds, kill them, mix their flesh together, and distribute their flesh to hills or mountains. After that He commanded Ibrahim to call the birds, and all the birds rose and flew towards Ibrahim. Quran 2 ayat 260:

Behold! Abraham said:

"My Lord! Show me how though gives life to the dead." He said: "Dost thou not then believe?" He said: "Year! But to satisfy my own understanding." He said: "Take four different birds; tame them to turn to thee; put a portion of them on every hill, and call to them; they will come to thee (flying), with speed. Then know that Allah is Exalted in Power, Wise."

Prophet Sulaiman (Solomon)

Allah gave Solomon miraculous gifts of powers such as great wisdom and knowledge, to command wind over to him; the control of devils and Jinns to obey him as an instrument of errand. He was able to listen to birds, fish, ants and other animals.

Quran 27:15-17:

And certainly, We gave knowledge to Dawood and Sulaiman, and both said: Praise to Allah, Who has made us to excel many of His believing servants.

And Sulaiman was Dawood's heir, and he said: O men! We have been taught the language of birds, and we have been given all things; most surely this is manifest grace.

And his host of the Jinn and the men and the birds were gathered to him, and they were formed into groups. What amazed Prophet Solomon was that an ant cried out to other ants that Solomon's army was coming and that the ants should hide in their homes so that the army would not step on them and kill them all. When Prophet Solomon heard this statement, he immediately asked Allah to teach him how to thank Him for the great blessing Allah had given to him and to do good deeds that will please Allah.

Surah Al Naml, Quran 27:15-19:

"We gave (in the past) knowledge to David and Solomon: and they both said: 'praise be to Allah, who has favored us above many of His servants who believe!"

And Solomon was David's heir. He said: "O ye people! We have been taught the speech of Birds, and we have been bestowed (a little) of all things: this indeed grace is manifest (from Allah)."

And before Solomon were marshalled his hosts—of Jinns and men birds, and they were all kept in order and ranks.

At length, when they came to a (lowly) valley of ants one of the ants said: "O ye ants, get into your habitations, lest Solomon and his hosts crush you (under foot) without knowing it."

So he smiled, amused at its speech; and he said: "O my Lord! So order me that I may be grateful for Thy favors, which Thou Hast bestowed on me and my parents and that I may work righteousness that will please Thee: and admit me, by Thy Grace, to the ranks of Thy Righteous servants."

When Prophet Solomon was with his people on his way home from performing the pilgrimage in Mecca and could not find the bird named Hoopoe, he was angry and threatened to punish him unless he gave a genuine reason for his whereabouts. Then the Hoopoe came and told Prophet Solomon of what he saw which the king had no knowledge of before. The bird said he had the news of a town called Sheba (Saba) in Yemen, which was being ruled by a queen named Bilikis (Bilqis). Solomon got the news about her from the Hoppe (Al Hudud) and wanted to invite her to Islam, he sent the bird to give her with the letter of invitation. Queen Bilikis responded to the invitation with a series of gifts to Solomon. Solomon considered these gifts to be a bribe and replied to her that: "I am well to do in my kingdom and all that I need from you is to obey and believe in the oneness of Allah, my Lord the Creator of the universe." If Bilikis disbelieves and fails to honor the invitation, her action might lead to war. She agreed to meet with Sulaiman, but before she got there Sulaiman had sent one of the Jinns to bring Queen Bilikis' chair to his palace. On arrival, Bilikis was surprised to see something similar to her majesty's chair in Solomon's palace. Solomon asked her to examine the chair if it was her chair, after thorough examination, she concluded that it was her chair. It was a miracle to her how it happened because the seat of Bilikis was in Yemen and Solomon's throne was in Palestine two thousand miles apart. And for the seat to be there in the twinkle of an eye became a misery not only to the Queen but to those who were with Solomon. That was another power of miracle given to Solomon and Bilikis accepted Islam.

When we talk about miracle, Jesus was not the first prophet to perform miracle. Allah gave miracles to other prophets as well. The chair of Queen Bilikis was removed from Yemen to Solomon's palace in Palestine within a second was a great miracle and the people at that time did not associate or attached this miracle to the power of Prophet Solomon (Alayhi Salam) as the Christians did to Jesus Christ (pbuh).

Read more from Quran chapter 27 verses 15-44:
Prophet Daud (David, AS).

Allah also gave him knowledge and wisdom and commanded the mountains and birds to celebrate with him and gave power to cast iron in any shape or form.

Prophet Idris (Enoch, AS).

Prophet Enoch was the first prophet after Adam. He was famous for honesty, sincerity and patience.

He and his followers raised their hands towards the sky in prayer and Allah revealed upon Idris that he had been selected as His Messenger. Allah also told him that all the reward He bestowed upon the whole world, He would give the same reward to him alone. Prophet Enouch was so happy about this news, and he wanted this reward to continue forever. Since he used to interact with the angels, he narrated Allah's promise to them and asked the angels to plead with Asarail—the angel of death, to not kill him. As another angel was taking him from earth to heaven, Allah instructed the angel of death to take his soul to the fourth heaven. When the angel and Prophet Enouch (Idris) ascended to fourth heaven, they met Asarail, the angel of death; the angel told Asarail that he had a visitor who wanted to meet with you with a request of preserving his life. Asarail asked the angel where was the visitor, he answered, "He is on my back and his name is Prophet Idris (Enoch)." Asarail said, "Allah just told me to take his life when he got to the fourth heaven and I was wondering how he would get here." At fourth heaven, the angel of death took his soul.

Surah Maryam, Quran 19:56-57:

"Also mentioned in the Book the case of Idris: He was a man of truth (and sincerity), (and) a prophet:

"And We raised him to a lofty station."

Since people did not witness his death, the Christians believe he is still alive and that he is the only human being who never died including Jesus (Isa). This is a wrong impression by the Christians. The Holy Quran chapters 5:117, 3:144 and 21:34 disputed the Christians' account.
Quran chapter 5:117 says:

"Never said I to them aught except what Thou didst command me to say, to wit, 'worship Allah, my Lord and your Lord'; and I was a witness over them whilst I dwelt amongst them: when thou didst take me up thou wast the Watcher over them, and Thou art a witness to all things."

Quran Chapter 3:144 says:

Muhammad is no more than a Messenger: many were the Messengers that passed away before him. If he died or was slain, will ye then turn back on your heels? If any did turn back on his heels, not the least harm will he do to Allah; but Allah (on the other hand) Will swiftly reward those who (serve him) with gratitude.

Quran chapter 21:34-35 says:

We granted not to any man before thee permanent life (Here): if then thou shouldst die, would they live permanently?

Every soul shall have a taste of death: And We test you by evil and by good by way of trial. To the US must ye return.

These quotations from the Holy Quran have put to rest that Jesus is alive in heaven and he is coming back to life again.

All the souls of righteous people including Prophets are alive in heaven until the judgment day when the soul and body will join together again for eternity.

Finally, let us quickly examine this Surah Al-Hadid, Quran 57: 1-6 and see if Jesus performed this miracle before he was born, when he was in her mother's womb and when he was eventually born and who was in control?

1 – Whatever is in the heavens and on earth, declares: The Praises and Glory of Allah: for He is the Exalted in Might, the Wise.

2 – To Him belongs the dominion of heavens and the

earth: It is He Who gives Life and Death; and He Has Power over all things.

3 – He is the First and the Last, the Evident and the Hidden: And He has full knowledge of all things.

4 – He is Who created the heavens and earth in six Days, then He established Himself on the Throne. He knows what enters within the earth and what comes forth out of it, what comes down from heaven and what mounts up to it. And He is with you wheresoever ye may be. And Allah sees well all that ye do.

5 – To Him belongs the dominion of heaven and earth: and all affairs go back to Allah.

6 – He merges Night into Day, and He merges Day into night; and He has full knowledge of the secrets of (all) hearts.

Was Jesus (pbuh) have powers to do all the above except the Almighty Allah (God).

Dear readers, if even with the miracles performed by previous prophets, with the permission of Allah, their followers did not attribute these powers to qualify them to be sons of God or God himself, how come the Christians attribute the miracles of Jesus to something else!

Chapter 13

The Crucifixion of Jesus

There is another area of confusion that we need to shed some more light on: the crucifixion of Jesus Christ, because most Christians believe that Jesus was crucified.

The readers would wonder or be surprised that the author is making references to the Holy Quran most of the time. I am using the Quran because it is the last revelation given to the last Prophet Muhammad (saw) and Allah gave him the account of all that had happened and the changes which human beings had made to previous scriptures to misguide people by concealing the truth for their personal gains.

The Christians believe that Prophet Isa (Jesus Christ) was crucified, but Allah said in the Holy Quran Surah Nisai (Quran 4 ayat 157-159):

157 – That they said (in boast). "We killed Christ Jesus, the son of Mary; the Messenger of Allah." But they killed him not, nor crucified him. But so it was made to appear to them, and those who differ, therein are full of doubts. With no (certain) knowledge, but only conjecture to follow, for of a surety—they killed him not.

158 – "Nay Allah raised him up unto Himself; and Allah is Exalted in Power, Wise—

159 – "And there is none of the people of the Book but must believe in him before his death; and on the Day of Judgment, he will be a witness against them."

Here Allah said We made it appear he was crucified and that is why the Bible did not have an accurate time of his death. (Mark 15:25)

"And it was the third hour, and they crucified him." (John 19:14-15)

14 – "And it was the preparation of the Passover, and about the sixth hour: and he saith unto the Jews, Behold your King,

15 – "But they cried out, away with him, away with him, crucified him."

(Matthew 27:45-46).

45 – "Now about the sixth hour there was darkness over all the land unto the ninth hour.

46 – "And about the ninth hour Jesus cried with a loud voice, ELI, ELI, LAMA SABACHTANI? My God, my God, why hast thou forsaken me?"

We can now see that Mark, John and Matthew were not able to give precise time because they all ran away and were not there only to listen to hearsay. But Allah brought Jesus to the world in a miraculous way, and he went back to Allah in a miraculous way as well. And if Jesus was crucified, where was he buried?

Let us refresh our memory a little bit on how Jesus came to the world as an individual human being.

First, the angels gave Mary glad tidings that she would have a baby. But she questioned. "How can I have a child when no man has touched me?" The angel replied that that is the power of God "Be, and it will be."

Second, the birth of Jesus was by miracle. Jesus has a mother but no father; this is the power of God. He gave Jesus tremendous and enormous powers to perform miracles to convince the Bani Israel (the Israelites) and idol worshippers at that time that there's a supernatural being that created you and the universe including what you created yourself and worship.

Third, when the disciples asked Jesus to ask God to send down food; Surah Al Maida, Quran 5:112-115:

112 – Behold! The Disciples said: "O Jesus the son of Mary! Can thy Lord send down to us a table set (with viands) from heaven?" Said Jesus: "Fear Allah, if ye have faith."

113 – They said: "We only wish to eat thereof and satisfy our hearts, and to know that thou have indeed told us the truth; and that we ourselves may be witnesses to the miracle."

114 – Said Jesus the son of Mary: "O Allah our Lord! Send us from heaven a table set (with viands), that there may be for us—for the first and the last of us—a solemn festival and a sign from Thee; and provide for our sustenance, for Thou art the best sustainer (of our needs)."

115 – Allah said: "I will send it down unto you; but if any of you after that resist faith, I will punish him with a

penalty such as I have not inflicted on anyone among all the peoples."

Fourth, but when the Pharisees plot to kill Jesus, God put the image of Jesus unto one of the plotters who was nailed on the cross. And God took him (Jesus) back to heaven. This was not clear to the Christians. The division among the Christians began from this moment as some groups believed and some didn't.

Some Muslims believe that Prophet Isa (Jesus pbuh) was not crucified but raised to heaven by God and he is coming back towards the end of the world to complete his work, marry, have children and die like other previous prophets and human beings. This was also supported by a Christian theologian in his Gospel of Basilides. He was a great scholar who had taught in Alexandria, Egypt, in the second quarter of the second century (C-185 – C254). But let us be clear about this ambiguity, Jesus is dead and is not coming back. The Holy Quran set the record straight on these issues.

1 – Surah Al Ahzab, Quran 33:40, "Muhammad is not the father of (any) one of your men, but (he is) the Messenger of Allah and the last of the Prophets. And Allah has full knowledge of all things."

2 – Surah Al Ambiyai, Quran 21:34: "We granted not to any man before the permanent life (Here): If then thou shouldst die, would they live permanently?"

3 – Surah Al Maidah Quran 5:117: "I was a witness over them whilst I dwelt amongst them; when thou didst take me up thoust wast the watcher over them, and thou art a witness to all things."

4 – Surah Al Imran, Quran, 3:144. "Muhammad is no more than a Messenger: many were the Messengers that passed away before him."

This evidence put to rest the questions of Jesus' death and his coming back to the world again.

The Christians have said that Jesus is the only son of God whom God sent to come and die for the sins of the world! But consider these points: Jesus said himself, he didn't come to die or sacrifice. (Matthew 9:13).

> "But go ye and learn what that meaneth, 'I will have mercy, and not sacrifice: for I am not come to call the righteous, but sinners to repentance."

How can God sacrifice His only child for the sins committed by others?

If the only son (Jesus) died for world sins, therefore, there shouldn't be any sin committed by anyone in this world again.

That means, the world is free from sins and no sinners go to hell fire. In contradiction to the above statement, the Bible says in Galatians 6:5:

> "For every man shall bear his own burden." In Ezekiel 18:20:

> "The soul that sinneth, it shall die. The son shall not bear the iniquity of the father; neither shall the father bear the iniquity of the son. The righteousness of the righteous shall be upon him, and the wickedness of the wicked shall be upon him."

In the Holy Quran, the following chapters 6:164, 17:15, 35:18, 39:7 and 53:38 all supported the Bible assertions that, "no bearer of burdens can bear the burden of another."

The Christians also believe that Jesus is God himself, who came in the flesh of a human being! But how could God subject Himself into the womb of Mary eating food and feeding on placenta? And he was born like other human beings, eating food, wearing clothes, taking showers, going to the toilet and sleeping?

In Luke 2:21:

21 – "And when eight days were accomplished for the circumcision of the child, his name was called JESUS, which was the name of the angel before he was conceived in the womb."

In Luke 11:27:

27 – "And it came to pass, as he spoke these things, a certain woman of the company lift up her voice, and said unto him, Blessed is the womb that bare thee, and the paps which thou hast sucked."

In these two chapters, how can God be circumcised on the 8th day and sucked his mother's breast?

When he was in his mother's womb (Mary's belly/stomach) who was in control of the world's affairs, the mountain, the ocean, feeding fish, the earth, taking care of animals, and the sky? When I asked these questions from my Christian friends, they could not give me any tangible or credible answers except to say that "I cannot understand." Of course, I can never understand them for I only understand what Allah says in the Holy Quran, 2:255; that He (God) doesn't sleep!

God has created angels whom He assigned to protect every individual and to record their deeds as He says in Surah Al-Infitar, Quran 82:10-11:

"But verily over you (are appointed angels) to protect you." "Kind and honorable writing down (your deeds)."

So whenever the author asks his friends again about the

whereabouts of the angels God created for protection on the day that He (God) Himself or his son was on the cross to be crucified, they usually have no sensible answer.

There is total confusion here between Christians' contention that Jesus is God himself, and Jesus is the son of God. On the day they claim that Jesus was crucified, they also say that Jesus was calling his Father God. Luke 23:46:

"And when Jesus had cried with a loud voice, he said, Father, into thy hands I command my spirit: and having said that, he gave up the ghost."

Matthew 27:46: And about the ninth hour Jesus cried with a loud voice, saying, ELI, ELI, LAMA SABACHTHANI? That is, My God, My God, why hast thou forsaken me?

Now, how can the person who is the one and only God call upon a higher power than himself to rescue and save him? In this case, it is an insult to the intelligence of Christians to say God came in the form of a human being.

The fact that God says that He created human beings in His own image does not mean He came to the world in a human form. Remember what God told Moses when Moses requested to see Him because God was talking to Moses directly. God said, "You will never see me because no eyes have ever seen God, and no eyes will ever see God." When Moses insisted, He told him that if the mountain can withstand the light I am sending to the mountain, then you can see me. But when the light came and the mountain crumbled, Moses passed out, becoming unconscious. When Moses regained himself, he repented and asked Allah for forgiveness and promised that he would never do it again (Surah Al A'raf-Quran Chapter 7 verse 143). This shows that no one can describe God, but we can describe Jesus.

Jesus himself gave different accounts in the Bible because he is not a God but a servant of God. I don't know what confused the Christians, why have they continued to embellish human beings like them beyond his human flesh. Let us examine critically with an open mind what Jesus (PBUH) said with his own mouth in the Bible.

REFERENCES FROM THE BIBLE

With all the confusion as who Jesus (Peace be upon him) was, as some Christians claimed he was the son of God, Holy Spirit or God himself who came in the form of a human being. (Holy Trinity); Let us examine what Jesus (Pbuh) said from his own mouth as stated from the Bible.

EVIDENCES IN THE BIBLE THAT JESUS (PBUH) WAS NOT A GOD

1 – (John 8:42) "Jesus said unto them, If God were your Father, ye would love me: for I proceeded forth and came from God; neither came I of myself, but He sent me." (That means, Jesus was a man and a messenger.)

2 – (Luke 18:19) "And Jesus said unto him. Why callest thou me good? None is good, save one, that is, God." (That means, no one is "God" including Jesus. Only God is "God.")

3 – (John 20:17) "Jesus saith unto her, touch me not; for I am not yet ascended to my Father: but go to my brethren, and say unto them, I ascend unto my Father, and your Father; and to my God, and your God." (That means, we all have one God.)

4 – (Mark 12:29) "And Jesus answered him, 'The first of all the commandments is, Hear, O Israel; The Lord our God is one Lord.'" (That means our God is one God.)

5 – (John 14:28) "Ye have heard how I said unto you, I go away and come again unto you. If ye loved me, ye would rejoice, because I said, I go unto the Father: for my Father is greater than I." (That means the God Almighty is Greater than Jesus.)

6 – (Numbers 23:19) "God is not a man, that he should lie; neither the son of man, that he should repent." (That means Jesus had categorically denied he is not God or son of God.)

7 – (John 4:24-26).

24 – Jesus said, "God is a Spirit, and they that worship Him must worship him in spirit and in truth.

25 – "The woman saith unto him, I know that Messiah's cometh, which is called Christ: when he is come, he will tell us all things.

26 – "Jesus saith unto her, 'I that speak unto thee am he." (Jesus is making it clear that no one can see God, but people saw Jesus because he was a human being.)

8 – (Habakkuk 1:12) "Art thou not from everlasting, O Lord my God, mine Holy One." (That means, God is the living and everlasting.)

9 – (Malachi 3:6) "For I am the Lord, I change not." (That means God Doesn't change His Nature.)

10 – (Ezekiel 20:20) "And hallow my Sabbaths; and they shall be a sign between me and you, that ye may

know that I am the Lord your God." (God Declared Himself to be God, but Jesus didn't.)

11 – (Matthew 26:39) "And he went a little further, and fell on his face, and prayed, saying, 'O my Father, if it be possible, let this cup pass from me: nevertheless, not as I will, but as thou wilt." (If Jesus were to be God, which God was he praying to?)

The TEMPTATION OF JESUS IN THE WILDERNESS BY SATAN (Devil).(Matthew 4:1-11)

1 – Then was "Jesus led up the Spirit into the wilderness to be tempted by the devil.

2 – "And when he had fasted forty days and forty nights, he was afterward a hungered.

3 – "And when the tempter came to him, he said, if thou be the Son of God, command that these stones be made bread.

4 – "But he answered and said, It is written, Man shall not live by bread alone, but by every word that proceedeth out of the mouth of God.

5 – "Then the devil taketh him up into the holy city, and setteth him on a pinnacle of the temple,

6 – "And saith unto him, if thou be the Son of God, cast thyself down: for it is written, He shall give his angels charge concerning thee: and in their hands they shall bear thee up, lest at any time thou dash

thy foot against a stone.

7 – "Jesus said unto him, it is written again, 'thou shall not tempt the Lord thy God.'

8 – "Again, the devil taketh him up into an exceeding high mountain, and sheweth him all the kingdoms of the world, and the glory of them.

9 – "And saith unto him, all these things will I give thee, if thou will fall down and worship me.

10 – "Then saith Jesus unto him, Get thee hence, Satan: for it is written, 'Thou shalt worship the Lord thy God, and he only shalt thou serve.'

11 – "Then the devil leaveth him, and behold, angels came and ministered unto him." (This shows Jesus was tempted as a man, while God cannot be tempted.)

EVIDENCES IN THE BIBLE THAT JESUS (PBUH) WAS A PROPHET

The people of Jerusalem recognized Jesus as a prophet and Jesus did not deny that. A prophet sent by God.

2 – (Mark 6:4), "But Jesus said unto them, 'A prophet is not without honour, but in his own country, and among his own kin, and in his own house." (Jesus also confirmed that he was a prophet.)

3 – (Mark 9:37), "Whosoever shall receive one of such children in my name, receiveth me: and whosoever

shall receive me, receiveth not me, but Him that sent me." (This is another attestation by Jesus himself that he was a prophet.)

4 – (Luke 7:16), "And there came a fear on all: and they glorified God, saying, 'That a great prophet is risen up among us'; and 'That God hath visited his people."

5 – (John 6:14), "Then those men, when they had seen the miracle that Jesus did, said, this is of a truth 'that prophet that should come into the world."

1 – (Matthew 21:10-11).

10 – "And when he had come into Jerusalem, all the city was moved, saying, Who is this?

11 – "And multitude said, "This is Jesus, the prophet of Nazareth of Galilee."

ACCORDING TO THE BIBLE JESUS (PBUH) CALLED HIMSELF A (SON OF MAN)

1 – (Matthew 8:20), "And Jesus saith unto him, The foxes have holes, and the birds of the air have nests; but the son of man hath not where to lay his head."

2 – (Matthew 17:22), "And while they abode in Galilee, Jesus said unto them, The son of man shall be betrayed into the hands of men."

3 – (Matthew 18:11), "For the son of man has come to save that which was lost."

4 – (Luke 9:22), "Saying, 'The Son of man must suffer many things, and be rejected by the elders and chief priests and scribes, and be slain, and be raised on the third day."

5 – (1 John 5:27), "And hath given him authority to execute judgment also, because he is the Son of man."

BASED ON THE BIBLE JESUS (PBUH) REFERRED TO HIMSELF AS SERVANT/SLAVE

– (John 13:16), "Verily, verily, I say unto you, 'The servant is not greater than his lord; neither is he that is sent greater than he that sent him."

– (Matthew 10:24), "The disciple is not above his master, nor the servant above his lord."

JESUS SAID HIS REAL MISSION WAS TO PREACH, NOT TO SACRIFICE.

(Matthew 9:13),

"But go ye and learn what that meaneth, 'I will have mercy, and not sacrifice: for I am not come to call the righteous, but sinners to repentance."

If the Christians disagree with what their master said in his own words how we can be surprised with the confusion that plagues Christendom. The Christians believe more in Apostle Paul, who was not among Jesus' disciples but wrote 13 chapters of the Bible than Jesus himself.

Based on the public debates I had watched on the internet, between Sheik Ahmad Deedah, Sheik Yusuf Adepoju and Ustaz Jamiu Adegunwa and Christian pastors, you will be amazed with the answers given below by the pastors and reverends.

Let us look at some confusion of the Christians with their arithmetical calculations:

$$2 + 2 = 5, \text{ just as } 1 + 1 + 1 = 1$$

Please pay close attention and make your own judgment with what Prophet Jesus (PBUH) said earlier on and what the pastors said.

Who is God? Jesus.
Is Jesus the son of Mary? Yes.
Who created Mary? God.
Who is God? Jesus.
Is Jesus the begotten son? Yes.
Who is his father? God.
Who is God? Jesus.
Did Jesus die on the cross? Yes.
Who resurrected him? God.
Who is God? Jesus.
Did Jesus worship while on earth? Yes. Whom
did he worship? God.
Who is God? Jesus.
Did God have a beginning? No....
Then who was born on 25 December? Jesus. Who is
God? Jesus.
Where's God? In heaven.
How many are there in heaven? Only one God.
Where's Jesus? He is seated at the right hand of his father. Who is
God? Jesus.

Then how many are they in heaven? Only one God. Then how many seats? One.
Where's Jesus? Seated next to God. Then how are they seated? On one chair.
It's only understood by those with the Holy Spirit. Who is God? Jesus.

Hmm! When did the idea that God became man begin and how? The idea that God became man begin from Apostle Paul as stated in the Bible, 1 Timothy 3:16
And without controversy great is the mystery of godliness: God was manifest in the flesh, justified in the Spirit, seen of angel, preached unto the gentiles, believed on in the world, / received up into glory.
What confusion! It is so beautiful to be a Muslim, Allah (SWT), have mercy on us all and grant us His straight path so as not to go astray.

The Christians know this story, but surprisingly, they still claim that Jesus is the God Himself, who came in a human flesh. That is why God is angry with the Christians and Jews.

The circumstances surrounding Jesus; Crucifixion have brought division among his followers.

Finally, Allah said in the Holy Quran, Surah Al Furqan (Quran 25 ayah 20):

"And We never sent before you (Muhammad) any of the Messengers but verily they ate food and walked in the market."

That means, Jesus cannot be God because we saw him, he ate food, wore clothes, took showers and slept like every other human being. But Allah or God does not do all of the above.

CHAPTER 14

The Twelve Tribes of Israel

Whenever we discuss the twelve tribes of Israel or the children of God, many of us are not clear who they are. This prompted me to try to explain and clarify the twelve tribes of Israel and why God sent Prophets to them.

The twelve tribes of Israel according to the Bible are named after the twelve's sons of the Patriarch Jacob:

1-Reuben: Eldest son of Jacob, according to the Bible.

2- Simeon: Jacob's second son.

3- Levi: The third son of Jacob, known for his role as the priestly tribe.

4- Judah: Jacob's fourth son, from whom the kings of Israel descended.

5- Dan: Jacob's fifth son.

6- Naphtali: Jacob's sixth son.

7- Gad: Jacob's seventh son

8- Asher: Jacob's eight son.

9- Issachar: Jacob's ninth son.

10- Zebulun: Jacob's tenth son.

11- Joseph: (whose descendants formed Ephraim and Manasseh) and

12- Benjamin: (Jacob's youngest son, from whom King Saul, the first king of Israel,descended.

The above information can be found in 1 Chronicles 2:1-2

These twelve tribes of Israel were the one Allah (God)

commanded Moses (Musa pbuh) to save from prosecution of Pharaoh in Egypt.

Prophet Moses and his brother Aaron took the journey and Pharaoh, and his army chased them. When Pharaoh was about to catch up with them, at the Red Sea, the Israelites were terrified.

God commanded Moses to use his staff. The red sea splitted into two; Moses and his followers walked safely to the other side while God drawn Pharaoh with his forces.

As the journey continued, the children of Israel were thirsty in the desert on their way to the promised land; they started questioning Prophet Moses (pbuh). Moses beseech God for help and God assisted by letting him perform another miracle which strengthened his prophethood.

In Exodus 17: 1-7, The gushing of water from the rock.

1 – And all the congregation of the children of Israel journeyed from the wilderness of Sin, after their journey, according to the commandment of their LORD, and pitched in Rephidim: and there was no water for the people to drink.

2 – Wherefore the people did chide with Moses, and said, give us water that we may drink. And Moses said to them, Why chide you with me? Wherefore do ye tempt the LORD?

3 – And the people thirsted there for water; and the people murmured against Moses, and said, Wherefore is this that thou hast brought us up out of Egypt, to kill us and our children and our cattle with thirst?

4 – And Moses cried unto the LORD, saying, what shall I do unto these people? They be almost ready

to stone me.

5 – And the LORD said unto Moses, Go on before the people, and take with thee of the elders of Israel; and thy rod, wherewith thou smotest the river, take in thine hand, and go.

6 – Behold, I will stand before thee there upon the rock in Horeb; and thou shalt smite the rock, and there shall come water out of it that the people may drink. And Moses did so in the sight of the elders of Israel.

7 – And he called the of the place Massah, and Meribah, because of the chiding of the children of Israel, and because they tempted the LORD, saying, Is the LORD amongst us, or not?

Based on the above information in the Bible, let us examine critically how the holy The Quran simplifies it to be more understood or clarity.

In Surah Al A'raf, Quran 7:160 - We divided them into twelve Tribes or nations. We directed Moses by inspiration, when his (thirsty) people asked him for water: "Strike the rock with thy staff": out of it there gushed forth twelve springs:

Each group knew its own place for water. We gave them the shade of the clouds, and sent down to them manna and quails, (saying): Eat of the good things we have provided for you".

(But they rebelled); to Us they did no harm, but they harmed their own souls.

Allah makes it clear to us that the twelve children of Jacob (Yaqub) are the twelve tribes of Israel. Each one of them has their own spring of water to drink to avoid commotion and confusion. These twelve tribes that Allah purposely asked Moses and his brother

Aaron to take care of, he provided for them and saved them from persecution in the hands of Pharaoh in Egypt.

Let us observe one thing here. First, Allah asked Moses to use his staff to swallow Pharaoh Magicians' materials. Second, Allah instructed Moses to use his staff to divide Red sea as a pathway for these twelve tribes to save and lead them to the promised land.

And thirdly, it was this same staff of Moses that Allah commanded Moses to strike the rock from which twelve springs of water gushed out to quench their thirst. Despite all these miracles performed by Moses through Allah's leave, these tribes still disobeyed God.

The Jesus Christ (pbuh), the son of Mary, was another prophet that God sent to the same people and to nobody else. Indeed, Jesus said categorically that, "I was sent only to the lost sheep of the house of Israel." Mathew 15: 24

In Matthew 10:5-6, Jesus instructed his disciples and said:

5 – To these twelve tribes, Jesus was sent. he commanded them saying: "Go not into the way of the Gentiles (non-Jewish), and into any city of the Samaritans enter ye not:

6 – But, go rather to the lost sheep of the house of Israel.

This was Jesus' mission ordained by the Almighty God. He would not transgress the order of Almighty God. This also confirmed that Jesus was not sent to the whole world but strictly to the Jewish people.

Chapter 15

The Story of Apostle Paul

This is the story of Apostle Paul, who originally was called Saul of Tarsus. Born in Cilicia in today's Turkey in 4 B.C., Paul is considered the second most powerful figure in Christian religion after Jesus Christ, peace be upon him. Paul was not among the twelve disciples of Jesus (pbuh) and he never met Jesus during his lifetime. Apostle Paul used to persecute the followers of Jesus until God turned his life around and started to obey God. Paul wrote 13 chapters out of 27 of the New Testament. Seven of the letters were authentically dictated by him, while the other six were accredited to him by his followers. Saint Paul constantly used information in Acts as a source, which is mostly a direct contradiction to his letters. The seven chapters written by Paul are Romans, 1 Corinthians, 2 Corinthians, Galatians, Philippians, 1 Thessalonians, and Philemon. The six written in his name by his followers after his death are: Ephesians, Colossians, and 2 Thessalonians, 1 and 2 Timothy.

Paul, Jewish and a Greek- speaker. During his youthful life, he learned how to work with his hands (1 Corinthians 4:12), and specialized in making tenet as a profession which he continued to do after his conversion to Christianity. He loved to travel from place to place and he can easily set up a shop with a few leather tools anywhere he might be. Paul knew how to dictate and he could write with his own hand in bold letters (Galatians 6:11) and could not write in neat small letters as a professional writer could. Paul was a member of the Pharisees, a religious group that sprang up during the later Second Temple period, when he was at the midpoint of his life. Pharisees believed in life after death, which was one of Paul's deepest convictions. The Pharisees embraced non biblical traditions as important as the written Bible. Pharisees were very careful students of the Hebrew Bible, and Paul was able to quote massively from the Greek translation; Paul referred to his expertise in "tradition" (Galatians 1:14). As a young ambitious and intellectual man, he memorized the Bible as he foresaw into the future how difficult it would be to carry around dozens of bulky scrolls. Paul credited himself as the best Jew and the best Pharisees of his generation (Philippians 3:4-6; Galatians 1:13-14). He later claimed to be the best apostle of Christ (2 Corinthians 11: 22-31;Corinthians 15:9-10), although he gave his excellent attribute to the grace of God.

As mentioned earlier, in persecuting Christians, Paul believed that Jewish converts to the new religion were not adequately observant of the Jewish law, and that Jewish converts interacted too freely with the Gentile (non-Jewish) converts, which he considered an abomination, which could lead to associating themselves with idolatrous practices, or regarding the crucifixion of Jesus as questionable. "The young Paul certainly doubted that Jesus was raised after his death, not because he did not believe in resurrection, but because he doubted that God chose to favor Jesus by raising him before the time of the judgment of the world."

According to some Pastors interpretation of the above quotation, when Paul was originally Saul of Tarus, he doubted the resurrection of Jesus and thought that God did favoritism to Jesus before the judgement day. He was anti-Jesus preaching at the time before he converted.

Paul's persecution of new converts among Jesus followers probably involved traveling from synagogue to synagogue and urging the punishment of Jews who accepted Jesus as the Messiah. Paul adopted ostracism or light flogging as a form of punishment to disobedient members of synagogues, which he too later suffered at least five times (2 Corinthians 11:24), but he did not say when and where. 87

According to Acts, Paul began his persecutions in Jerusalem, but he later denied that he knew any of the Jerusalem followers of Christ until after his own conversion (Galatians 1:4-17). Paul was traveling to Damascus when he had a vision that changed his life; according to Galatians 1:16, God revealed his son to him. More specifically, Paul stated that he saw the Lord (1 Corinthians 9:1), though Acts claimed that near Damascus he saw a bright blinding light. To some Reverends, Bishops and Pastors, Paul was blind for three days with no food or water when God was talking to him and this convinced Paul that God had indeed chosen Jesus to be the promised messiah. Then he went into Arabia—probably Coele-Syria, West of Damascus (Galatians 1:17); then returned to Damascus and three years later, he went to Jerusalem to be associated with the leading apostles there such as Peter and James. After his meeting, he set out on his missions to the west, preaching first in his hometown of Syria and Cilicia (Galatians 1:17-24). During the next twenty years, he established several Churches in Asia Minor and at least three in Europe, including the Church in Corinth.

Paul observed that his preaching to the Gentiles was creating more problems for the Christians in Jerusalem, who thought that Gentiles must become Jewish first before embracing Christian movement. To solve the problem, Paul returned to Jerusalem to make peace and struck a deal between the two camps. It was agreed that Peter would be the principal apostle to Jews while Paul would be the principal apostle to Gentiles. It was agreed that Paul did not need to change his message but he oversaw the collection of Jerusalem Church, which was in need of financial support (Galatians 2:1-10; 2 Corinthians 8-9; Romans 15:16-17, 25-26), though Paul's Churches could barely make ends meet. Paul interpreted the "offering" to his followers that they must come to Jerusalem with their wealth in hands as prophesied in Isiah 60:1-6. It was also obvious that Paul and the Jerusalem apostles made a political agreement not to interfere in each other's areas or backyard.

Paul's Mission: caused confusion to Christendom till today. Paul proclaimed that Jesus (pbuh) was the Messiah and son of God, and that he lived in heaven, and he would soon return. Paul revealed that God chose him purposely to the Gentiles (Galatians 1:16). By his last letter,

Romans, Paul clearly described his own place in God's plan. He wrote that Hebrew prophets had prophesied that in "days to come," God would restore the tribes of Israel and the Gentiles would return to worship a true God. Paul maintained that his purpose in this mission was to win over the Gentiles, both Greeks and "Barbarians" (the common language used for non-Greeks at the time) (Romans 1:14). Paul boastfully said, "In as much as I am an apostle to the Gentiles, I glorify my ministry in order to make my own people jealous and thus save some of them" (Romans 11:13- 14). He believed that Jews would eventually become Christian because of the successful mission of the Gentiles. Paul was known to be the authoritative apostle to the Gentiles. An unknown missionary established a church in Rome before Paul's arrival and Paul viewed some of them as competitors. He treated some nicely while he viewed other preachers with suspicion and called some Christians in Jerusalem hypocrites.

What Paul add to Christianity

1 – Paul's basic message was about death, resurrection, and lordship of Jesus Christ and declared that having faith in Jesus' guarantees share in his life. It was Paul who reminded the Galatians and Romans in his letter that "It was before their eyes that Jesus was crucified and that his death was a benefit to the believers because he sacrificed his life to wipe out the sins of human-being. Jesus never said that his death will wipe out their sins.

This is Paul's own statement to brainwash his followers that Jesus died for their sins.

(Galatians 3:1, 1 Corinthians and Romans 3: 23-25). And that Jesus died so the believers can live with him.

– It was Paul who first advocated for total celibacy: That is, "it is better for a man not to touch a woman" (1 Corinthians 7:1). Nuns and fathers especially in the Catholic faith.

– It was also Paul who advocated that members must obey their secular rulers because their powers came from God, and they must submit to the will of the rulers no matter how unjust they were. And disobedience carries severe punishment.

– From the beginning, Jesus had only one name, "Jesus"; he was referred to as "Jesus from Nazareth" (Matthew 21:11), "Joseph's son" (Luke 4:22) or "Jesus son of Joseph from Nazareth" (John 1:45). It was Paul who renamed Jesus as Christ, son of God and Messiah (Romans 6:4). Jesus never did.

– It was Paul who proclaimed that Jesus Christ was pre-existing and came to earth in a human form. Jesus never did. The evidence is stated below.

In Philippians 2: 6-11

7-" who, being in the form of God, thought it not robbery to be With God"

8-But made himself of reputation, and took upon him the form of servant, and was made in the likeness of men:

9- And being found in fashion as a man, he humbled himself, and became obedient unto death, even the death of the cross.

10-Wherefore God also hath highly exalted him, and given him a name which is above every name:

11-That at the name of Jesus every knee should bow, of things in heaven, and things in earth, and things under thee.

12- And that every tongue should confess that Jesus Christ is Lord, to the glory of God the father.

13-According to the Bible, Jesus was sent to the twelve tribes of Israelites, which himself confirmed. But it was Paul who started to preach that God sent Jesus to save the whole world.

14- It was Paul who named his followers Christians. Jesus (pbuh) never did.

15- It was Paul who established churches. Jesus (pbuh) never did and was opposed to it.

In Mark 16:15

"And he said unto them, go ye into all the world, and preach the gospel to every creature." But Jesus never did.

Bishop Bruce, a friend of mine from Citizen Police Academy confirmed that Jesus (pbuh) did not establish any physical church, but he was preaching from place to place and that was what he instructed his disciples to do. He further stated that church is supposed to be like an institution (university) where students learn and spread the gospel, and not a place of congregation as witnessed today. Bishop Bruce cited the example of himself standing in a corner of the street preaching gospel to the people.

Bishop Bruce supported the above statement from the Bible Acts 7: 48

"Howbeit the most High dwelt not in temples made with hands; as saith the prophet". But Bishop Bruce interpreted this way: (The house of worship is a gathering where others come together in acknowledging one another, and the true living God. But always remember, that God resides in you. It does not reside in human hands.

My dear readers, in his efforts to serve God, have a place in history, and outshine other disciples, Paul introduced and imposed his own ideology onto the religion, while sometimes contradicting himself and this has created problems for today's Christians.

Note: Jesus' symbol when he was alive was fish and not Cross. It was during the reign of Emperor Constantine in the 4th Century when he converted to Christianity and the cross was promoted as the symbol of the son of God.

The story of Saint Paul was extracted from the article written by E.P. Sanders: https://www.britannica.com/biography/Saint-Paul-the-Apostle.

Chapter 16

Al-Islam

I know that many people or authors have defined Islam in as many ways as they see fit. According to Malise Ruthven, "Islam is a religion of peace: the word Islam, a verbal noun meaning submission (to God), is etymologically related to the word Salam, meaning peace." The standard greeting most Muslims use when joining a gathering, meeting strangers or meeting each other is "As-salaam alaikum," "peace be upon you." But I am going further in my own definition as to what Islam entails.

Islam means peace. The religion of Islam is the religion of peace. An Islamic greeting is mandatory by Allah. Surah Al Noor, Quran 24 ayat 27: "O you who believe! Do not enter houses other than your own houses until you have asked permission and saluted their inmates: this is better for you, that you may be mindful." Surah 24, ayah 61 says: "When you enter houses, greet your people with salutation from Allah, blessed (and goodly, thus does Allah make clear to you the communications that you may understand." This is different from other greetings which have no meaning such as "good morning, good afternoon, good evening or goodnight." But greeting in Islam is a prayer of goodwill permitted by Almighty Allah (SWT) who makes its return compulsory or obligatory upon the person or people it is said to. Failure to return it becomes a sin in the sight of Allah.

Asalaam alaikum, short form that is—peace be unto you! The respondent must say, Wa Alaikum, Salaam—peace be upon you too. But Allah makes it mandatory for the respondent to give his or her return in full. That is to say, "Wa'alaikum Salaam Warahmatullahi,

Wabarakatuhu." Meaning, peace and the blessing of Allah be upon you. Surah Al-Nissai, 4, ayah 86 says: "When you are greeted with a greeting, greet with a better (greeting) than it or return it; surely Allah takes account of all things."

Based upon this divine instruction on ethics and morals, Muslims deem it fit to extend or exchange salutation among themselves.

Islam is total submission to the Will of Almighty Allah (The Creator of the Universe and what is in heaven and earth). When we use the word submission, it means to obey Allah (SWT) in totality, follow what He commands us to do and abandon what He dislikes no matter whether or not that dislike is beneficial to you/ us. There's no picking and choosing in Allah's injunctions.

Islam is not just a religion but a way of life. Islam teaches the oneness of God, the unseen God, who gave the signs of His existence through His creations. Islam also teaches that there's no deity of worship except the Almighty Allah. Islam teaches us how to relate to Allah in terms of faith and to deal with ourselves. Islam teaches the benefits of obeying Allah and the consequences of disobedience. Islam also teaches us to depend and rely solely on Allah in good times and bad times. In one of the hadiths of the Prophet Muhammed (PBUH) Hadith # 9 of Fortieth Hadith/ Hadith Nabawi, narrated by Ibn Abbas. He said, one day, he was behind the noble Prophet who told him:

> "O young boy, I will teach you some words: Guard
> Allah's commandments and He will guard you. Guard
> Allah's commandments, you will find Him in front of
> you. If you ask, then ask Allah, and if you seek help,
> then seek help from Allah and know that if the whole
> world was to gather to help you, they would never be
> able to help you except with something which Allah
> has already decreed for you. And if the whole world
> gathers to cause you some harm, they would not be

able to harm you except with something which Allah has already preordained for you. The pens have been lifted, and the scrolls have dried" (Trimidhi).

This hadith indicates to human beings and Jinns that only Allah (SWT) deserves relying upon in all our affairs. Allah will never renege in His promise as He said in Surah Al Imran, Quran 3, ayah 9. Human beings change their promises and are therefore unreliable. But Allah will always stand by you if you have faith in Him.

Islam is the only religion that Allah has chosen for mankind and Jinn. Quran 3, ayah 19. Allah also said that whoever practices another religion than Islam, He would not accept it and on the day of judgment, the person will be a loser (Quran 3 ayah 85). There's a unity in one religion. If we observe Muslims all over the world, we can see that any Muslim can worship in any Masjid that is available regardless of race, color, origin or nationality. Why? The Quran is one, the prayers (Salats) are the same and the language of prayer is one, which is Arabic language. Upon the completion of the congregational salat, an individual resorts to his or her local language or dialect for personal request from Allah. This is the beauty and uniqueness of religion. Islam brings bond among its adherents all over the world. According to what Allah Subuhanahu Wa Ta'ala said in the Holy Quran, Surah 49, ayah 10: "The believers are but brothers and sisters." And this was supported by the Holy Prophet Muhammad (PBUH) in one of the hadiths: "A Muslim to another Muslim is like a brother or sisters to another."

Hadith # 35 page 112 of An-Nawawis of Forty Hadith translated by Ezzeddin Ibrahim and Denys Johnson-Davies.

Islam encourages its followers to give people their rights regardless of their faiths. It also permits people to do good to their family, neighbors, orphans, coworkers and wayfarers, whether they are Muslims or not.

It goes further that animals must be given their rights as well. That means animals cannot be maltreated.

In the medieval era, women were not recognized. They were regarded as second fiddles, used in ritual sacrifices to gods, and denied of their due inheritance. They were not allowed to get education but to remain as housewives and slaves. But it was Islam who gave liberation to women, and the Western world hijacked the advocacy of these rights from Muslim and took credit for it. Islam gives respect and honor to women. In the Holy Quran, chapter four is dedicated to women (Surah Al Nisai). The Prophet Muhammad (SAW) in one of his hadiths related by Trimidhi said: "The best of you are the best of you towards their wives." The Holy Quran surah 46 ayat 15, "We have enjoined on man kindness to his parents: In pain did his mother bear him, and in pain did she give him birth." The carrying of the (child) to his weaning is a period of thirty months. At length, when he reaches the age of full strength and attains forty years, he says, "O my Lord! Grant me that I may be grateful for thy favor which thou have bestowed upon me, and upon both my parents, and that I may work righteousness such as thou mayest approve: and be gracious to me in my issue. Truly have I turned to Thee and truly do I bow (to Thee) in Islam." This ayah also emphasized that women, especially the mothers, should be given more respect because the development of human beings starts from women's womb until delivery stage, breastfeeding and until weaning period till adulthood is not an easy job. That is why the prophet (Pbuh) said, the paradise of an individual is at the heel of his/her mother. A man asked Prophet Muhammed (SAW), "To whom deserves to be treated righteously?" He said, "Your mother." The man asked, "Who's next," he said, "Your mother." The man asked again, "Who's next?" The Prophet said, "Your mother." The man asked again, "Who's next?" The prophet answered, "Your father." This hadith was narrated by Bukhari. Hadith # 5626 and Muslim hadith # 2548 Book 32 # 6180 from

Kitab Al-Birr was Adas. The Book of virtue, good manners and joining of the Ties of Relationship, chapter 1- politeness towards parents and their Right to it.

Women and men are equal in the sight of Almighty Allah, although Allah gives each different role or responsibility. Allah does not create a separate paradise or hellfire for men and women, both will enter the same paradise as well as the same hellfire.

Islam forbids Muslims to act unjustly towards non-Muslims. Muslims must protect them including their wealth and they must not oppress them or transgress upon them or deprive them of their rights. Muslims must be nice to non-Muslims regardless of their religion, race, color, national origin or gender.

When I spoke with my Christian friends and some pastors as why Christians cannot worship in other churches apart from their own denomination, the answer was lengthy but just to summarize it here. They said each sect or denomination of Christians would like to worship of their own because of differences in structure and doctrine, although they all believe in Jesus Christ and each follows the doctrine of their leaders. They gave the example that Catholics started the Christian religion and when they did not practice it the way some Christians see it; they protested it and broke away and they were called Protestant; then Anglican, Methodist, Baptist and so and so forth until Jehovah's witnesses, etc., every group was breaking away for one reason or another. And because of these differences in worship and structure that is why they cannot worship together.

According to my own experience and observation when my friends were pressuring me to join them, I went to so many churches to observe the way they worship and observed that each church conduct their services differently according to their own rules and regulations which are not similar to others unlike Muslims whereby you can worship in any mosque regardless of who establish that mosque because it the same way of worship in America is the same way in China or Europe based on the same Quran. But nearly each sect of Christianity has their own Bible interpreted into the way of their worship.

There are some churches whose members can see vision to any member during service and start speaking strange languages that no one understands except some who interpret the message and you wonder, where does the vision or revelation come from?

I also asked some of the pastors that Jesus did not sing, clap and dance during worship in the New Testament, how come that Christians today who call themselves the followers of Jesus worship differently from their Master? There were no coherent answers. Some said singing and dancing was in the Old Testament and the youth of today wanted to inculcate ideas that will attract their colleagues to churches.

Finally, In Surah Al Imran, Quran 3: 102. Allah said:
"Oye who believe!
Fear Allah as He should be feared and die not except in a state of Islam.

This is to show that this is the only religion empowered by Allah for every human-being and no one returns to Him without embracing or practicing this particular / specific religion as He has stated in several chapters of the Quran.

Five Pillars of Islam as in the Bible

There are five pillars of Islam.

1– Shahadah – To believe that there's no deity of worship but Almighty Allah, and that Prophet Muhammad is a servant of Allah and His messenger. This means: no association of partners with Allah the Supreme Being. That every human being must obey His command which carries reward and disobedience leads to severe punishment. In addition, every human being and Jinn must follow the Sunnah of His messenger—the prophet Muhammed (PBUH).

By expressing and sincerely uttering this phrase, one becomes a Muslim. This is called: Declaration of faith.

According to the Bible (Mark 12:29). The great Commandment:

Jesus (pbuh) said: "The first of all the Commandment is "Hear O Israel; The Lord our God is one Lord."

2 – Salat: To worship Allah five times a day. To worship Allah is the most important duty that every human being and Jinn must do daily at its appointed time. Allah said our purpose of creation in this world is to worship Him. Quran 51:56.

Praying Salat is direct communication with your Lord without intervention. Ask Allah what you want and seek forgiveness with Him unlike the Christians who must confess their sins to their pastors. Some churches worship Saints (a human being) that passed away whom they choose among themselves that he /she answered their prayers when they pray to him or her. But you don't see that in Islam.

In (Matthew 26:39)

(Jesus) went a little further, "and fell on his face and prayed." Through Salat-daily prayers, Muslims communicate directly with God.

3 – Zakat: To give alms from our wealth to the needy. That is, human beings must not be niggardly or stingy towards another fellow. Part with what Allah has bestowed upon you no matter how small it is.

(Charity) Hebrew 13:16

Do not neglect to do good and to share what you have, for such sacrifices are pleasing to God.

Read more: Act 20:35, Matthew 6:1-4, Proverbs: 19:17, Luke 21:1-4 and Hebrew 13:2.

4 – Fasting according to the holy Quran Surah Al Baqarah,Q2:183
183 – O ye who believe!
Fasting is prescribed to you as it was prescribed to those before you, that ye may (learn) self-restraint.

Fasting: To fast in the month of Ramadan is mandatory for every human being and Jinn. The best month of the year is fasting for 29 or 30 days depending on the citation of the moon. And there's one night in this month which is called the "Night of Power." The benefit of this is equal to one thousand months. But the Prophet (PBUH) said that we seek this night during the last ten days of Ramadan, from 21st to 30th.

Fast in Islam teaches Muslims how to discipline themselves and develop spiritually. Fast is to abstain from food, drink, sex, smoking from dawn to sunset. There are exceptions for the sick, elderly and some women and travelers.

Matthew 6:16-18

16 – Moreover, when ye fast, be not as the hypocrites, of a sad countenance: for they disfigure their faces, that they may appear into men too fast. Verily I say unto you, they have their reward.

17 – But thou, when thou fastest, anoint thine head, and wash thy face;

18 – That thou appear not unto men fast, but unto thy Father which is in secret: and thy Father, which seeth in secret, shall reward thee openly.

The Christians now have different types of fasting according to the choice of their leaders and not according to their prophets. This is the explanation given to me by some pastors who've said Jesus fasted for forty days and forty nights and none of the Christians can fast like that. But today some churches fast for 60 days, 40 days, 21 days and some fast fewer days, while many churches are not fasting at all. Unlike Muslims all over the world who always observe the month of Ramadan, prepare and broadcast the beginning and ending of fasting with fanfare and celebration.

5 – Hajj: To perform pilgrimage to Makkah, the holy land in Saudi Arabia. The gathering of Muslims all over the world during the last month of Islamic Calendar year shows what the judgment day will look like. A Muslim is required to do this once in his /her life.

(Psalm 84:5-6)

5 – "Blessed is the man whose strength is in thee; In whose heart are the ways of them

6 – Who passing through the valley of Baca make it a well;"

The Baca here is referred to as Mecca or Makkah in Saudi Arabia.

This is to buttress that the religion of God is one religion and that is submission to the will of Almighty God. There's no ambiguity in it as it was in the beginning, now and forever.
All true and practical Muslims observe these five pillars wherever they are regardless of whether they are Sunnis or Shiites or Arab or non-Arabs, White or Black.
Theirs is not in the Bible or Torah where pilgrimage to Jerusalem was mentioned except the invention of the Jews and the Christians.

Let us look at this Devine law in Torah and the Bible, Exodus 21:10 and Quran 4:3

In the Bible: Exodus 21:10

10 – "If he takes him another wife; her food, her raiment, and her duty of marriage, shall he not diminish.

That means, you cannot deny her of her conjugal right. You have to serve them equally or stay with one wife otherwise you will be punished by God for injustice,

In Surah Al-Nisai: Quran 4: 3

3 – " If ye fear that ye shall not be able to deal justly with the orphans, marry women of your choice, two,

three or four; but if ye fear that ye shall not be able to deal justly (with them), then only one, orThat which your right hands possess, that will be more suitable, to prevent you from doing injustice".

It is the same law in the Torah and the Bible, but no Pastor or Reverend or Bishop ever educate their members of marrying more than one wife as permissible by God only to castigate the doer as infidelity.

However, they do propaganda of one man one wife whereas they permitted fornication / concubine adultery outside their marriage. While the Quran publicly addresses this issue of permissibility whoever can afford it.

This is to buttress that the religion of God is one religion and that is submissive to the will of Almighty God. There's no ambiguity in it as it was in the beginning, now and forever.

Chapt er 17

Jesus Was a Muslim

This may be a shocking revelation to a lot of Christians. Majority of them may doubt this fact and dispute the account because of what they have been made to believe that he (Jesus) is the son of God or God himself. But few Christians know the fact from the beginning, but they hide it because of what they may lose in financial profit or personal aggrandizement if they should let the cat out of the bag, they then conceal the truth and continue to mislead their congregations or followers.

It is not only Jesus that was a Muslim among the previous prophets; all the prophets were indeed Muslims.

Allah says in the Holy Quran chapter 42:13.

> "The same religion has He established for you as that which He enjoined on Noah—that which We have sent by inspiration to thee—and that which We enjoined on Abraham, Moses, and Jesus: namely, that ye should remain steadfast in Religion, and make no divisions therein: To those who worship other things from Allah, hard is the (way) which thou call them. Allah chooses whom He pleases, and guides to Himself those who turn (to him)."

All the prophets prayed as today's Muslims pray. The only difference is that they did not pray or worship five times daily because Allah (SWT) had not yet completed the religion of Islam; Islam was completed during the time of Prophet Muhammad (PBUH).

Jesus made wudu (ablution).

Before a Muslim prays, he must first do what is called ablution. That is the purification of the body whereby some parts of the body are washed; such as hands, mouth, nose, face, and the two arms from the wrist to elbow, head, ears and feet. During the times of the previous prophets, including Isa (Jesus), baptism and washing of feet were in the form of the Muslims' ablution. Jesus did this to his disciples and encouraged them to do it to others before entering the temple. The Jews also did the same before entering their synagogue as was likewise done by Prophets Moses and Aaron. In the Bible (Acts 21:26) ablution is the form of purification and a preparation for entering holy places.

After the ablution, the purification of the body with a clean cloth and a clean place, Jesus raised his hands up just like Muslims (Takberat L'Ihram) Allah Akbar—Allah is the greatest (1 Timothy 2:8);

"I will therefore pray that men pray everywhere, lifting up holy hands, without wrath and doubting."

In Leviticus 9:22:

"And Aaron lifted up his hands towards the people, and blessed them, and came down from offering of the sin offering, and the burnt offering, and peace offerings."

In Exodus 17:11:

> "And it came to pass, when Moses held up his hands, that Israel prevailed: and when he let down his hands, Amalek prevailed."

In Deuteronomy 32:40:

> "I lift up my hands to heaven, and say, I live forever."

Muslims bow to God in their prayers. Jesus
and other prophets did the same.

Not only did Jesus bow, he prostrated as well, just like Muslims do in their prayers.

In the Bible (Matthew 26:39):

> "And he (Jesus) went a little further, and fell on his face, and prayed, saying, 'O my Father, if it be possible, let this cup pass from me: nevertheless, not as I will, but as thou wilt."

In Matthew 17:6:

> "And when the disciples heard it, they fell on their face and were sorely afraid."

In Genesis 17:3:

"And Abraham fell on his face, and God talked with him, saying… In Exodus 34:8:

"And Moses made haste, and bowed his head toward the earth, and worshipped."

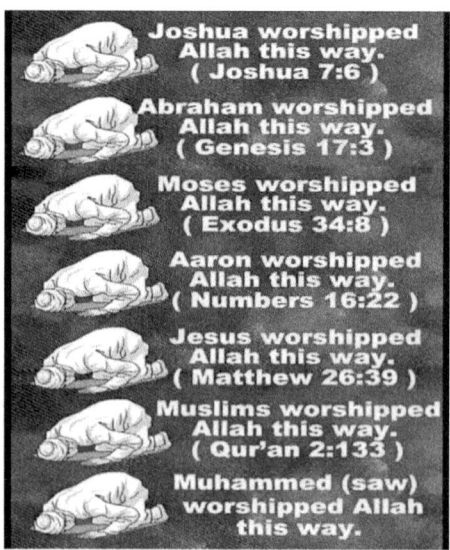

Joshua worshipped Allah this way.
(Joshua 7:6)

Abraham worshipped Allah this way.
(Genesis 17:3)

Moses worshipped Allah this way.
(Exodus 34:8)

Aaron worshipped Allah this way.
(Numbers 16:22)

Jesus worshipped Allah this way.
(Matthew 26:39)

Muslims worshipped Allah this way.
(Qur'an 2:133)

Muhammed (saw) worshipped Allah this way.

Nehemiah 8:4-6

4 – "And Ezra the scribe stood upon a pulpit of wood, which they had made for the purpose; and beside him stood Mattithiah, and Shema, and Anaiah, and Urijah, and Hilkiah, and Maaseiah, on his right hand; and on his left hand, Pedaiah, and Mishael, and Malchiah, and Hashum, and Hash- badana, Zechariah, and Meshullam.

5 – "And Ezra opened the book in the sight of all the people; (for he was above all the people ;) and when he opened it, all the people stood up:

6 – "And Ezra blessed the LORD, the great God. And all the people answered, Amen, Amen, with lifting up their hands: and they bowed their heads and worshiped the LORD with their faces to the ground."

This is the typical example of how Muslims worship Allah. In Surah Al Hajj, Quran 22 Ayat 77:

77 – "O ye who believe! Bow down, prostrate yourselves, and adore your Lord: and do good; that ye may prosper."

Muslims form a straight line and are led by the Imam. Then they will raise their hands up. When the Imam finishes the recitation of Surah 1 (Alfatiah) the congregation will answer (Ameen). And then proceed to bow down and prostrate. But the Christians suppressed this form of worship from the Bible.

There are other references in the Bible on the prostrations of other prophets when they prayed to God. In Surah Maryam (Mary), Quran – Chapter 19:58:

> 58 – "Those were some of the prophets on whom Allah did bestow His Grace of the posterity of Adam, and those whom We carried (in the Ark) with Noah, and of the posterity of Abraham and Israel—of those whom We guided and chose; whenever the ayat—signs of (Allah) Most Gracious were rehearsed to them, they would fall down in prostrate adoration and tears."

Let us compare the congregational prayer of the previous prophets in the Bible and Torah with that of al-Fatiah in the Quran, we can see that they are almost the same.

OUR LORD'S PRAYER

"OUR FATHER, WHO ART IN HEAVEN,

HALLOWED BE THY NAME,
THY KINGDOM COME,
THY WILL BE DONE, ON EARTH AS IT IS IN
HEAVEN, GIVE US THIS DAY OUR DAILY BREAD,
AND FORGIVE US OUR TRESPASSES,
AS WE FORGIVE THOSE WHO TRESPASS AGAINST
US. AND LEAD US NOT INTO TEMPTATION,
BUT DELIVER US FROM EVIL (AMEN)."

The prayer of the first chapter in the Holy Quran, SURAH AL FATIHAH, goes like this:

IN THE NAME OF ALLAH, MOST GRACIOUS, MOST
MERCIFUL. PRAISE BE TO ALLAH, THE CHERISHER

AND SUSTAINER OF THE WORLD;
MOST GRACIOUS, MOST MERCIFUL; MASTER OF
THE DAY OF JUDGMENT.
THEE DO WE WORSHIP, AND THINE AID WE SEEK.
SHOW US THE STRAIGHT WAY,
THE WAY OF THOSE ON WHOM THOU HAST
BESTOWED THY GRACE, THOSE WHOSE (portion) IS
NOT WRATH, AND WHO GO NOT ASTRAY (AMEEN).

After that the leaders and the congregants bow and then go to prostration until the completion of the prayer. This shows the religion of God is one.

If we have all these overwhelming proofs and evidence in the Bible that Prophet Isa (Jesus) prayed like Muslims, why are the Christians denying and shying away from the truth that Jesus was indeed a Muslim?

Jesus never prayed with eyes closed, did night vigils, collected tithes or went to church on Sunday.

And the irony of it all is that the Christians refuse to associate Jesus with Islam—total submission to the Will of Almighty God.

Furthermore, Jesus Christ never called his followers Christians just like Prophet Muhammad never called his followers Muhammadans. His followers, as followers of other Prophets, were called Muslims on the tongue of Prophet Ibrahim, and Allah approved of that name. Quran 22:77-78. Again, it was never mentioned in the bible that Jesus established a church or prayed in a church like prophet Muhammad (PBUH) established a Mosque upon his arrival in Medina, Saudi Arabia.

Finally, it was never mentioned in the Bible that Jesus worshiped his Lord by way of singing, dancing and clapping, where did his followers inherit this from if they are sincere followers of the New Testament.

Religion of God Is One; Al-Islam

God is one and the religion of God is one. All the prophets from Adam to Muhammad (May the peace of Allah be upon them all) preached the same oneness of Allah (God) and of religion which is Al-Islam. Allah makes it crystal clear in the Holy Quran, Surah Al Baqarah (2 ayah 213). "Mankind was one single nation, and Allah sent Messengers with glad tidings and warnings; and with them He sent The Book in truth, to judge between people in matters wherein they differ; but the people of the Book, after the clear signs came to them, did not differ among themselves, except through selfish contumacy.

> "Allah by His grace guided the believers to the truth, concerning that wherein they differed. For Allah guides whom He wills to a path that is straight."

Islam means total submission to the will of Almighty Allah. That is, to follow Allah's injunctions without reservations, and to distance ourselves away from what He forbids for us. If we do this, we will have peace in our life. But in His infinite love for us, Allah has made the practice of this religion (Al-Islam) the easiest for us by sending its pillars and tenets to us bit- by-bit until its total completion through the mission of the last prophet, Muhammad (SAW). That is to say, Religion of Islam was completed during the life of Prophet Muhammad (PBUH).

Previous Prophets were also worshiping and praising Allah in the morning and evening by way of praying, witness the Psalms of David. As part of His completion and perfection of His religion for the whole of mankind and Jinn, Allah sent Angel Jibril (Gabriel) to come and pick up Prophet Muhammed from earth to heaven. This is called (Al-Isra Wal- Miraj); the night journey from the Grand Mosque in Makkah (Al-Haram) to Masjid Al-Aqsa (the Holy

Sanctuary) in Jerusalem, and the ascension to heaven. On his way through heaven, Prophet Muhammad met some of the previous prophets starting from the first heaven where he met Adam, second heaven where he met John the Baptist (Yahya) and Jesus (Isa), third heaven where he met Joseph (Yusuf), fourth heaven where he met Enoch (Idris) fifth heaven where he saw Aaron (Harun), sixth heaven where he met Moses (Musa), and seventh heaven where he met Abraham (Ibrahim). When Angel Jibril (Gabriel) reached Sidratul-Muntaha he said, "I cannot go further than this place"; then the exchange of greetings between Prophet Muhammad and Allah transpired, with the angels sharing in the blessings.

"Attahiyyaatu Lillaah, Azzaakiyyaatu Lillaah, Atayyibaatu Salawaatu Lillaah, Assalaam 'Alaika Ayyuha Nnabiyyu Warahmatullaah Wabarakaatuhu. Assalaamu 'Alainaa, Wa 'Alaa 'Ibaadillaahi Ssaaliheena."

Meaning:

All greetings are due to Allah, All reverences are due to Allah, All sanctities are due to Allah, All worships are due to Allah.

Peace be upon you, O the Prophet (Muhammad), And Allah's peace and His blessings.
Peace be unto us (Angels) too, and unto the righteous servants of Allah.

At first, Allah gave to the Prophet fifty (50) prayers to be performed daily by Muslims. But it was due to the intervention of Prophet Musa (Moses), who advised Prophet Muhammad to go back to Allah and get them reduced because his followers will not be able to do fifty prayers daily based on his own experience with the Israelites.

Thus, Prophet Muhammad continued to go back and forth for reduction until Allah reduced it to five (5) prayers per day. Even these five were still too much for Prophet Musa (Moses), but Prophet Muhammad told him that he was too ashamed to go back to Allah for any further reduction. "We shall be okay with these five prayers," Prophet Muhammad said to his brother, Prophet Musa. Allah promised to give a reward of fifty for the performance of these five, and then Prophet Muhammad descended back to earth.

The Quran was revealed to the Prophet piecemeal for twenty-three (23) years. In it, Allah gave him the accounts of what had happened before the beginning of time to the present and what will happen in the future until the end of the world. At the end of its revelation, this is what Allah said in the Holy Quran Surah Al-Maida, Chapter 5:3, alluding to the completion and perfection of Islam:

"This day I have perfected your religion for you, completed my favor upon you, and have chosen for you Islam as your religion."

For that reason, Islam is the only religion Allah has ordained, chosen, commanded for all human-beings and the Jinns (Spirits). To the Christians and Jews, if your leaders (Prophets) have practiced Islam, why are you, the followers, practicing other religions than the one practiced by your masters? Both Moses and Jesus greeted people just like Muslims. The Jews will say "Shalom," meaning peace to you and Jesus also greeted with "peace be unto you," while Muslims greet with "Assalaam 'Alaikum," also meaning peace be upon you. One can now see that the greetings of the three religions are the same.

Therefore, if any of you, the followers of Moses and Jesus, refuses to obey and follow the religion of your Prophets (Islam), that person will just be wasting time; Allah gives warning in the Holy Quran to this effect. Surah Al Imran, Chapter 3:85:

"If anyone desires a religion other than Islam (submission to Allah), *never will it be accepted by him or her*, and in the hereafter, he or she will be in the ranks of those who have lost (all spiritual good)."

Dear fellow human beings, Allah has spoken and has given His verdict. Therefore, I am calling on you Christians and Jews to quickly return to the right path Allah has charted for you in the religion of Islam. And those of you who are practicing other religions than Islam such as Hinduism, Taoism, Confucianism, Cherubim and Seraphim, Jehovah's Witnesses, Seventh-Day Adventists, etc.; I can only appeal to you that it is not too late for you to embrace Islam. The founders of your religions are not Prophets with scriptures from God. Rather, they were leaders of their own ideologies and philosophies. They have brainwashed you in their philosophical doctrines which cannot save them nor help you on the Day of Judgment.

To support Islam as the only true religion for mankind ordained by Almighty Allah, read the quotes of some of the great Western Philosophers:

1 – Leo Tolstoy (1828-1910):

> "Islam will rule the world one day, because in it there is a combination of knowledge and wisdom."

2 – Herbert Wells (1846-1946):

> "Until the effectiveness of Islam again, how many generations will suffer atrocities and life will be cut off, then one day the whole world will be attracted to it, on that day there will

be Dilshad and on that day the world will be inhabited."

3 – Albert Einstein (1879-1955):

"I understand that Muslims did it through their own intelligence and awareness which the Jews could not do. In Islam it is the power that can lead to peace."

4 – Huston Smith (1919):

"The faith which is upon us, and this is better than us in the world, then it is Islam. If we open our hearts and minds for it, then it will be good for us."

5 – Michael Nostradamus (1503-1566):

"Islam will be the ruling religion in Europe, but the famous city of Europe will become the Islamic state capital."

6 – Bertrand Russell (1872-1970):

"I read Islam and realized that it is to be the religion of all the world and all humanity. Islam will spread through Europe and in Europe the big thinkers of Islam will emerge. One day it will come that Islam will be the real stimulus of the world." His prediction is happening today.

7 – Gosta Le Bon (1841-1931):

"Islam only talks about peace and reconciliation. Invite Christians to appreciate the faith of reform."

8 – Bernard Shaw (1856-1950):

"The whole world will accept Islam religion one day and if it cannot even accept the real name, it will accept it by the name of metaphor. The West will accept Islam one day and Islam will be the religion of those who have studied in the world."

9 – Johann Geith (1749-1832):

"We all must accept Islam religion of Islam sooner or later. This is the real religion. If I am called a Muslim, I will not feel bad, I will accept this right thing."

Source: https://steemit.com/religion/@yeanca07/quotes-regarding-islam- by-some-western-philosophers.

Allah says in the Holy Quran; Surah Al Imran Chapter 3:103:

"O ye who believe! Fear Allah as He should be feared and die not except in a state of Islam."

Allah also said in Surah Al Maidah, Quran 5 ayat 15-16:

"O people of the Scripture (Jews and Christians)! Now has come to you Our Messenger explaining to you much of that which you used to hide from the Scripture and pass over (i.e. leaving out without explaining) much. Indeed, there has come to you from Allah a light and a plain Book (this Quran). Wherewith Allah guides all those who seek His Good pleasure to ways of peace and brings them out of darkness by His Will unto light and guides them to the Straight Way."

And in Surah Al Taha- Quran 20 ayat 123-124:

"Then whoever follows My guidance, he shall neither go astray nor shall he be distressed. But whosoever turns away from My Reminder, verily for him is a life of hardship, and We shall raise him up blind on the Day of Resurrection."

And in Surah Fussilat- Quran 41 ayat 41-42:

"And verily, it is an honorable well-fortified respected Book. Falsehood cannot come to it from before it or behind it. (It is) sent down by the All-Wise, Worthy of all praise (Allah).

My fellow human beings, this is my fervent appeal to you. Get a copy of the Holy Quran and check out these facts for yourself, but with an open mind, and then make your decision whether it is worth continuing to be in the dark or to come to the light.

Chapter 18

The History of Prophet Muhammad (pbuh)

Prophet Muhammad was the last of all the prophets and their leader. Allah has sent him to be a warner to the Infidels and giver of good tidings to those who obey Allah's injunctions. He was also sent to all human beings and Jinns. We ask Almighty Allah to shower His blessings upon him, his household, his progeny and those who follow the religion of Islam until the Day of Judgment (Amen).

Before Prophet Muhammad came to this world, there was an interval of between 570-600 years after Jesus (PBUH). By then all the previous Holy Scriptures had been tampered with; a lot of injustices, oppressions, unnecessary killings, and denials to women of their inheritance, either from deceased parents or from deceased husbands. Baby girls were buried alive or killed for idol sacrifices or rituals. The world was shambled and chaos. There was clamoring for a new world order with a new leader with Divine intervention to sanitize and guide the world unto the straight path. And that was when Allah (SWT) sent Prophet Muhammed (SAW) to come to the world. But before he was born, there were some miracles that happened to which Muslims do not attach more importance than the message he brought to the world. The signs of universal changes during his birth just to mention a few are as follows:

1 – Satan was blocked from the news of the birth of the prophet

2 – Abraha from Abyssinia (Ethiopia) who wanted to destroy Kaaba and take over Mecca was destroyed by Allah who sent birds throwing stones from Hellfire at his army and killing all of them.

3 – The palace of the King of Persian (Kisra) was shaken and 14 balconies fell.

4 – The fire of Persia that had been burning for over 1000 years went off.

5 – The lake that ships used to sail dried up.

6 – The idols of Mecca were falling down, the biggest idol Hubba also fell.

7 – The devils were stricken with fallen stars.

After his birth, the draught that had been ravaging the land stopped; trees were germinating again, and cattle were producing milks.

Prophet Muhammad was born an orphan; his father Abdullah died six months before he was born, and at the age of six, his mother also passed away. According to Arab culture, when a child is born, he/she will be taken to a wet nurse who would breastfeed and nurture the child, and the Prophet (PBUH) was breastfed and nurtured by Halimah Saadiya.

One day, the Prophet (SAW) was playing with his peers, and a man came from nowhere and grabbed him. This was Angel Jibril (Gabriel) who came to cleanse him of evil thoughts. His peers ran away and informed Halimah (his foster mother) who was thereafter, so concerned for his safety that she returned him to his mother. Shortly after that his mother passed away and his grandfather, Abdul Muttalib became his guardian. Two years later, the grandfather also died. But while on his deathbed he entrusted the care of Muhammad to his son Abu Talib who was an uncle to the Prophet.

Being an orphan did not stop the prophet from moving on with his life. He was a shepherd, trader and caravan traveler with his uncle from Mecca to Bilad-Assham, now Syria, Jordan and Lebanon.

While on one of these trade journeys with his uncle, a Christian monk, Bahira, saw the prophet at Busra and saw a brighter future in Muhammad. He was also afraid that the Jews will try to harm him and thus advised Abu Talib to take him back to Mecca to protect him. As a youth, he was known to be truthful, honest and sincere and this earned him the nickname of "Al Ameen." He has mediated and settled crises among the tribes who are fighting to be the custodian of the holy site in Mecca. The prophet was in Mecca until when he was 25 years old when he made another business trip to Syria for a socialite woman in Mecca known as Khadija. When he returned from the trip and gave an accurate account of the trip in terms of both the capital investment and the profit, Khadija was amazed with his honesty and proposed marriage to him; she was 40 years old then. Both married and had seven children together; three males and four females. All the males died in their childhood.

At the age of 40, Muhammed's prophethood started, and his wife Khadija was the first to believe in him. He was preaching the oneness of Allah to the people of Mecca and telling them to worship God that created them rather than worshipping idols. This campaign did not go down well with these pagans of Mecca; they did not believe in the message of Muhammad to worship the unseen God. The Pagans plotted to assassinate him. God revealed their plan to him and asked him to leave Mecca for Medina. The Prophet and his close companion Abu Bakr left Mecca for Yathrib, later changed to Medina Al Munawara (the Illuminated city). The migration from Mecca to Medina is called Hijra which is the beginning of Muslims calendar. The Prophet was well received in Medina and he settled there.

Prophet Muhammad (PBUH) established a Mosque upon his arrival in Medina where he was directing and administering the affairs of Muslims. He had a cordial relationship with all ethnic groups in Medina. The news of his arrival spread like wildfire and the people around town and far away came to see him and submitted to his call to Allah. Before his arrival in Medina, the Medanites were preparing to install a Jewish man, Abdullah bin Ubay bin Saloul, the head of hypocrites as the King. Coincidentally, Prophet Muhammed arrived around this time, and his popularity with the people led to his being accepted as their leader instead of Abdullah ibn Ubay. Of course, Abdallah became very jealous and started to plot to harm the prophet, but he failed in his entire attempt.

However, the good behavior of Prophet Muhammed (SAW) and his conduct attracted more people to Islam. This is to the dismay of pagans of Mecca, from where many people were migrating to Medina to embrace the new religion of Islam. The pagans believed the only way to stop Prophet Muhammad (PBUH) and his new religion was to wage war against him and his followers. The Meccan pagans prepared one thousand soldiers to go and attack the Prophet in Medina, and the news of their impending attack came to the knowledge of the Prophet. Muslims at that time were very few; they could assemble only three hundred people, including the prophet himself, who participated in defending the new religion, relying on their Lord, Allah for help. Because this was a war of aggression, the three hundred Muslims defeated the army of the people of Makkah with the help of angels, whom Allah sent to help the Muslims in their first war, known as the battle of Badr. The victory of the Muslims gave them the confidence to practice their religion with complete freedom.

Allah (SWT) said, we gave the Prophet (PBUH) knowledge and

morals, and we asked him to teach the world the ethics and morals based on this, the prophet stopped the killing of females or burying them alive. He stopped the killing of human beings for sacrifice to the idols. He liberated women from oppression and gave them their rights in inheritance, divorce and equality between men and women.

The Prophet was a good father, good husband, good leader and good commander-in-chief. Allah said in Surah Al Ahzab, Quran, Chapter 33:21: "You have, indeed, in the Messenger of Allah a beautiful pattern (of conduct)." Therefore, emulate his good character and let him be your role model if you want to be the inheritor of this life and hereafter. Allah said, Prophet Muhammad was sent as a mercy for all His creatures.

Allah granted prophet Muhammed (pbuh) four magnificent special privileges which He has never promised or provided any prophets before him. They are as follows: Al-Wasilah, Al-Kawthar, Al-Hawdh, and Al- Maqam Al-Mahmud.

> 1 – "Al-Wasilah is the privilege/opportunity for the Messenger of Allah to intercede with Allah on the Day of Resurrection.
>
> 2 – "Al-Kawthar is a river in paradise for his followers.
>
> 3 – "Al-Hawdh is the water basin for his followers; once a Muslim drinks its water on the Day of Judgment he will never feel thirst again. And
>
> 4 – "Al Maqam Al-Mahmud is the praised station in the Here- after" (Minhaj A-Muslim Volume 1, page 63).

Prophet Muhammad (Pbuh) said, "Had either Musa (Moses) or Isa (Jesus) been alive, he would have no choice but to follow me." (Recorded by Abu Ya'la with different wording, Minhaj Al-Muslim,

Volume 1, page 56.)

The Prophet (Pbuh) never imposed his will on anyone if they disagreed with him. He never oppressed anyone or waged any war of aggression but wars of defense if attacked. He always preached peace and patience. He liberated women and gave them their rights. He collected zakat (the poor-due) from the rich to take care of the poor. He preached human rights, freedom of religion, freedom of assembly equality and good deeds among human beings regardless of race, color, gender or nationality. He opposed the killing of the innocent, unjust wars and animal cruelty. Most of his teachings were hijacked by the Western nations and adopted in their laws, while Muslim nations that are supposed to be the champions of his legacy are the ones that are backward in their own lifestyles.

Today, you may see some few extremists such as Al-Qaeda, ISIS, Boko Haram, Al-Shabab, Taliban, and the likes doing some crazy things under the pretext of Islam and misinterpreting some ayah of the Holy Quran to justify their stupid, evil and barbaric acts. Alas! Islam does not support their views and as a matter of fact, their views are contrary to the teachings of Islam.

What non-Muslims say about Prophet Muhammad (Pbuh).

1 – Napoleon Bonaparte – Quoted in *Christian Cherfils BONAPARTE ET ISLAM* (PARIS 1914):

"I hope the time is not far off when I shall be able to unite all the wise and educated men of all the countries and establish a uniform regime based on the principles of Qur'an which alone are true, and which alone can lead men to happiness."

2 – M. K. Gandhi, *YOUNG INDIA*, 1924

"...I became more than ever convinced that it was not the sword that won a place for Islam in those days in the scheme of life. It was the rigid simplicity, the utter self-effacement of the prophet, the scrupulous regard for his pledges, his intense devotion to his friends and followers, his intrepidity, his fearlessness, his absolute trust in God and his own mission. These, and not the sword carried everything before them and surmounted every trouble" (YOUNG INDIA, 1924).

3 – Lamartine – *Histoire de la Turquie*, Paris 1854, Vol II, pp. 276-77:

"If greatness of purpose, smallness of means, and astounding results are the three criteria of human genius, who could dare to compare any great man in modern history with Muhammad? The most famous men created arms, laws and empires only. They founded, if anything at all, no more than material powers which often crumbled away before their eyes. This man moved not only armies, legislations, empires, peoples and dynasties, but millions of men in one-third of the then inhabited world; and more than that, he moved the altars, the gods, the religions, the ideas, the beliefs and souls... the forbearance in victory, his ambition, which was entirely devoted to one idea and in no manner striving for an empire; his endless prayers, his mystic conversations with God, his death and his triumph after death; all these attest not to an imposture but to a firm conviction which gave him the power to restore a dogma. This dogma was two fold, the unit of God and the immateriality of God; the former telling what God is, the latter telling what God is not; the one overthrowing a false god with the sword, the other starting an idea with words.

"Philosopher, orator, apostle, legislator, warrior, conqueror of ideas, restorer of rational dogmas, of a cult without images; the founder of twenty terrestrial empires and of one spiritual empire, that is Muhammad. As regards all standards by which human greatness may be measured, we may well ask, is there any man greater than he?"

4 – Edward Gibbon and Simon Ocklay – *History of the Saracen Empire*, London, 1870, p. 54:

"It is not the propagation but the permanency of his religion that deserves our wonder, the same pure and perfect impression which he engraved at Mecca and Medina is preserved, after the revolutions of twelve centuries by the Indian, the African and the Turkish proselytes of the Koran...The Mohammedans have uniformly withstood the temptation of reducing the object of their faith and devotion to a level with the senses and imagination of man. 'I believe in One God and Muhammad the Apostle of God' is the simple and invariable profession of Islam. The intellectual image of the Deity has never been degraded by any visible idol; the honors of the prophet have never transgressed the measure of humanvirtue, and his living precepts have restrained the gratitude of his disciples within the bounds of reason and religion."

5– Rev. Bosworth Smith, Mohammed and Mohamadanism, London 1874,p.92

"He was Caesar and Pope in one; but he was Pope without Pope's pretensions, Caesar without the legions of Caesar: without a standing army, without a bodyguard, without a palace, without a fixed revenue; if ever any man had the right to say that he ruled by the right divine, it was Muhammad, for he had all the power without its instruments and without its supports."

6 – Annie Besant, *The Life and Teachings of Muhammad*, Madras 1932, p. 4:

"It is impossible for anyone who studies the life and character of the great Prophet of Arabia, who knows how he taught and how he lived, to feel anything but reverence for that mighty Prophet, one of the great messengers of the Supreme. And although in what I put to you I shall say many things which may be familiar to many, yet I myself feel whenever I re-read them, a new way of admiration, a new sense of reverence for that mighty Arabian teacher."

7 – Montgomery Watt, *Muhammad at Mecca*, Oxford 1953, p. 52:

"His readiness to undergo persecutions for his beliefs, the high moral character of the men who believed in him and looked up to him as leader, and the greatness of his ultimate achievement—all argue his fundamental integrity. To suppose Muhammad an impostor raises more problems than it solves. Moreover, none of the great figures of history is so poorly appreciated in the West as Muhammad."

8 – James A. Michener, "Islam: The Misunderstood Religion" in *Reader's Digest* (American Edition), May 1955, pp. 68-70:

"Muhammad, the inspired man who founded Islam, was born about A.D. 570 into an Arabian tribe that worshipped idols. Orphaned at birth, he was always particularly solicitous of the poor and needy, the widow and the orphan, the slave and the downtrodden. At twenty he was already a successful businessman and soon became director of camel caravans for a wealthy widow. When the Prophet was twenty-five-year-old, his employer, recognizing his merit, proposed marriage to him. Even though she was fifteen years older, he married her and remained a devoted husband.

"Like almost every major prophet before him, Muhammad fought shy of serving as the transmitter of God's word, sensing his own inadequacy. But the angel commanded 'Read.' So far as we know, Muhammad was unable to read or write, but he began to dictate those inspired words which would soon revolutionize a large segment of the earth: 'There is one God.'

"In all things Muhammad was profoundly practical. When his beloved son Ibrahim died, an eclipse occurred, and rumors of God's personal condolence quickly arose. Where- upon Muhammad is said to have announced, 'An eclipse is a phenomenon of nature. It is foolish to attribute such things to the death or birth of a human-being.'

"At Muhammad's own death an attempt was made to deify him, but the man who was to become his administrative successor killed the hysteria with one of the noblest speeches in religious history: 'If there are any among you who worshipped Muhammad, he is dead. But if it is God you worship, He lives forever.'"

9 – Michael H. Hart, *The 100: A Ranking of the Most Influential Persons in History*, New York: Hart Publishing Company, Inc. 1978, p. 33:

"My choice of Muhammad to lead the list of the world's most influential persons may surprise some readers and may be questioned by others, but he was the only man in history who was supremely successful on both the religious and secular level."

10 – Sarojini Naidu, the famous Indian poetess says – S. Naidu, Ideals of Islam, Speeches and Writings, Madaras, 1918

"It was the first religion that preached and practiced democracy; for, in the mosque, when the call for prayer is sounded and worshippers are gathered together, the democracy of Islam is embodied five times a day when the peasant and king kneel side by side and proclaim: 'God Alone is Great."

11 – Thomas Caryle – *Heroes and Heroes Worship*

"How could one man single-handedly weld warring tribes and Bedouins into a most powerful and civilized nation in less than two decades?"

"...The lies (Western slander) which well-meaning zeal has heaped round this man (Muhammed) are disgraceful to ourselves only...How one man single-handedly, could weld warring tribes and wandering Bedouins into a most powerful and civilized nation in less than two decades....A silent great soul, one of that who cannot but be earnest. He was to kindle the world; the world's Maker had ordered so."

12 – Stanley Lane-Poole – *Table Talk of the Prophet*

"He was the most faithful protector of those he protected, the sweetest and most agreeable in conversation. Those who saw him were suddenly filled with reverence; those who came near him loved him; they who described him would say, 'I have never seen his like either before or after.' He was of great taciturnity, but when he spoke it was with emphasis and de- liberation, and no one could forget what he said..."

13 – George Bernard Shaw – *The Genuine Islam* ,Vol. No. 8, 1936

"I believe if a man like him were to assume the dictatorship of the modern world, he would succeed in solving its problems in a way that would bring much needed peace and happiness. "I have studied him—the man and in my opinion is far from being an anti-Christ. He must be called the Savior of Humanity.

"I have prophesied about the faith of Muhammad that it would be acceptable in Europe of tomorrow as it is beginning to be acceptable in Europe of today."

Prophet Muhammad (Pbuh) said in one of his hadith said: "Had either Musa or Jesus (Peace be upon both) been alive, he would have no choice but to follow me" (recorded by Abu Ya'la) (*Minhaj Al-Muslim*), Volume: 1, page 56, by Abu Bakr Jabir Al-Jazairy).

Chapter 19

Holy Quran
What Is the Quran?

The Quran is the Holy book from the Almighty Allah, revealed to the prophet Muhammed through Angel Jibril as a guide to mankind and jinn so that they can know the right from wrong, and there will be judgment for every action. Surah Al Baqara, Quran 2, ayah 185. The Quran was revealed in Arabic language, the language of the Prophet Muhammed (pbuh) so that he can explain clearly to his people, Surah Ibrahim, Quran 14, ayah 4.

> "And We did not send any apostle but with the language of his people, so that he might explain to them clearly."

In another chapter of the Quran, Surah Yusuf 14, ayah 2:

> "Surely We have revealed it—an Arabic Quran—that you may understand."

Allah laid emphasis on the language of the Quran (Arabic) which is the language of the Prophet Muhammed so that people cannot say he did not understand the message of Allah if it was revealed in a different language.

This also indicates that the language of worshiping Allah is the Arabic language which Allah chooses for the world. And that is why Muslim can worship in any Mosque around the globe. In addition to that, it is the language on the day of judgment.

Under the promise of a prophet, the prophet Moses (pbuh) prophesied the coming of Jesus (pbuh) in Deuteronomy 18:15 states, "The Lord your God will raise up for you a prophet like me from among you, from fellow Israelites. You must listen to him."

The Jesus Chris (pbuh) also prophesied the arrival of the new scripture of the holy Quran which can also be found in the Bible 1Corinthians 13: 9-10

9 – "For we know in part, and we prophesy in part.

10 – "But when that which is perfect has come, then that which is in part shall be done away.

According to AMPC, Jesus talks about the Quran in the same 1Corintians 13: 9-13 that "For our knowledge is fragmentary (incomplete and imperfect), and our prophesy (our teaching) is fragmentary (incomplete and imperfect).

But when the complete and perfect (total) comes, the incomplete and imperfect will vanish away (become antiquated, void and superseded. https://www.bible.com

Most of all these information in the Bible, the pastors of the Churches were not educating their members or followers about the Quran and the prophet Muhammad; they hide the truth because of their own personal benefits and gains,

This is what prophet Isa (Jesus Pbuh) said about the Quran, the last revelation and the coming of the prophet Muhammad (pbuh) as the last prophet.

The Quran is the world constitution which every human being must follow as guidance for daily lives. The Quran was the last revelation, and no other scripture is coming after it. The Quran came to correct the previous scriptures which human beings have distorted, manipulated, edited, revised and changed several times. Allah gave the accurate account to the noble Prophet Muhammed (SAW). Allah said in the Surah Yusuf, Quran 12, ayah 111:

"There is, in their stories, instruction for men endued with understanding. It is not a tale invented, but a confirmation of what went before it, a detailed exposition of all things, and a Guide and Mercy to any such as belief."

Since its revelation, Allah is the one that protects the Quran from distortion as human beings have made several attempts to change it to confuse people. Human beings have not given up their attempts to manipulate the meaning of the original translation, but they will not succeed. Allah said in the Surah Al Hijr, Quran 15, ayah 9:

"We have, without doubt, sent down the message; and We will assuredly guard it (from corruption)."

The Uniqueness of the Holy Quran

Over 1,400 years that the Quran has been revealed, no one is yet to produce a single chapter. Despite that "Thomas Carlyle" in his lectures on Heroes and Hero worship of May 12, 1840, where he referred to the prophet Muhammad as POET. But Allah Subuhanahu Watala, challenged people like Thomas Carlyle in Surah Al Baqarah, Quran 2, ayah 23:

"And if you are in doubt as to what We have revealed from time to time to Our servant, then produce a surah like thereunto and call your witnesses or helpers (if there are any) besides Allah, if your (doubts) are true."

And in another Surah Al Isra-Quran 17 ayat 88:

"Say, if mankind and the Jinns were together to produce the like of this Qur'an, they could not produce the like therefore, even if they helped one another."

To support this, many men, women and children have memorized the whole of the Quran from the first page to the last page.

The Quran talks about life in this world and life in the hereafter and gives options for individuals to make his or her decision about paradise or hellfire. Surah Al Insan, Quran 76, ayah 3:

3 – "We showed him the Way: whether he be grateful or ungrateful (rests on his will)."

In the Quran, the stories of previous people were clearly narrated. The current science discovery, technological advancement and future discoveries have been revealed in the Quran over 1400 years ago to an unlettered prophet Muhammed (pbuh).

Support of Science in the Holy Quran

The Quran had talked about embryology, astronomy, oceanography, geology and metrology which were recently discovered through modern equipment. Surah Fussilat, Quran 41, ayah 53 says:

"Soon will We show them our signs in the (furthest) regions (of the earth), and in their own souls until it becomes clear to them that this is the Truth."

And the most fascinating aspect of it is the development of the human being from conception till delivery period. Surah Al Mu'minun, Quran 23, ayah 12 - 14 says:

12 – "We did create man from a quintessence (of clay);

13 – "Then We placed him as (a drop of) sperm in a place of rest, firmly fixed;

14 – "Then We made the sperm into a clot of congealed blood; then of that clot We made a (fetus) lump; then We made from that lump bones and clothed the bones with flesh; then We developed out of it another creature. So, bless be Allah, the best to create!"

The Beginning of Life

Allah let us know in the holy Quran that water (H2O) is the most needed element for life in the universe, which had been confirmed by scientific re- search. Surah Al Anbiya, Quran 21, ayah 30:

"Do not the unbelievers see that the heavens and the earth were joined together (as one unit of creation), before we clove them asunder? We made every living thing from water. Will they not then believe?"

The Enlargement of the Universe, Mountains, sky's protection, the benefit of Iron, the Sun's orbit and the internal waves in the ocean and many more scientific discoveries such as the Two Seas that do not mix, all have evidence in the holy Quran.

The Purpose of Holy Quran

The revelation of the Quran is to guide human beings and Jinns toward believing in One True God and to reject all false gods. Allah said in Surah Al Baqara, Quran 2, ayah 163 and Surah Al Nisai, Quran 4, ayah 36.

In Surah 2, ayah 163, Allah says:

"And your God is One God: There is no god but He, Most Gracious, Most merciful."

And in Surah Al Nisai 4, ayah 36:

"Serve Allah and join not any partners with Him...."

Since Allah is alone, there's no deity worthy of worship except Allah.

There's no Ambiguity in the Quran

When human beings write, there will be a mistake or mistakes either in the construction, phrase, grammar or spelling, incorrect facts, omissions and exaggerations and confusion. But that is not the case with the Quran because it came directly from Allah to the Prophet Muhammad (SAW). All accounts of events were accurate, be they relating to cosmology, water cycle, geology, scientific explanation, prophecies and embryology. Allah said in Surah Al Nisai, Quran 4, ayah 82:

"Do they not consider the Quran (with care)? Had it been from other than Allah, they would surely have found therein much discrepancy."

The Quran was not sent as a complete book but was revealed in bits for the period of 23 years; 13 years in Makkah and 10 years in Medina.

Chapter 20

Evidence of Universal Religion in Islam

The Bible had prophesied the universal religion of Islam as we can see in Revelation 14: 6-7

> 6 – " And I saw another angel fly in the midst of heaven, having everlasting gospel to preach unto them that dwell on the earth, and to every nation, and kindred, and tongue, and people,

> 7 – " Saying with a loud voice, "Fear God, and give glory to Him; for the hour of His judgement is come: and worship Him that made heaven, and earth, and the sea, and the fountains of waters."

The above revelation was that the last prophet will be sent to all nations, and they will worship God in one tongue that is one language which is Arabic language, the language of Al-Quran as Muslims all over the world are using today.

Islam is the only religion that Allah has ordained for the whole world; that is, it is the universal religion. As per Allah (SWT): "This day have I perfected for you your religion and completed My favor on you and chosen for you Islam as a religion" (Quran 5:3).

Then, in Quran 3:19, He says: "Surely the (true) religion with Allah is Islam, and those to whom the Book had been given did not show opposition but after knowledge had come to them, out of envy among themselves; and whosoever disbelieves in the communications of Allah then surely Allah is quick in reckoning."

Many Muslims all over the world pray five times daily.

All Muslims use one language to pray, which is Arabic. Quran 12:2, "Surely, We have revealed it—an Arabic Quran—that you may understand. Quran 42:7, "And thus have We revealed to you an Arabic Quran...."

The Holy Quran is the completion of all previous revelations such as Torah, Old Testament and New Testament.

Allah mentions the name of the Quran in the Holy Quran – Chapter 36:2, "I swear by the Quran full of wisdom."

Allah mentioned Islam in Quran – Chapter 3:19, "Surely the (true) religion with Allah is Islam." And in Quran, 3:85, He says: "And whoever desires a religion other than Islam, it shall not be accepted from him, and in the hereafter, he shall be looser."

Allah mentioned Muslims in the Quran – Chapter 3:102, "Do not die unless you are Muslims."

All Muslims face the Kaaba in Mecca during their prayers. Quran Chapter 2:149, "And from whatsoever place you come forth, turn your face towards the Sacred Mosque...."

I am calling your attention to observe Synagogues and churches in your area and see if they all face the same direction. You will not see it because there is nothing in the Torah or Bible that says so.

All Muslims fast in the month of Ramadan. Quran Chapter 2:185, "The month of Ramadan is that in which the Quran was revealed, so every one of you who is present (at his home) during that month should spend it in fasting...."

All Muslims have a common central Mosque—The Kaabah. And in every Muslim country, there is a central Mosque for all Muslims.

Many Muslims perform hajj at the same time of the year in Makkah, Saudi Arabia. Quran Chapter 2:197, "The Pilgrimage (hajj) is (performed in) the well-known months...."

Praying on Friday is ordained by Almighty Allah in Surah Al Jumah, Quran 62:9, "O you who believe! When the call is made for prayer on Friday, then hasten to the remembrance of Allah and leave off trading; that is better for you, if you know."

Does God ordain Jews in the Torah that Saturday is their holiest day for worship?

Does God ordain the Christians in the Bible that Sunday is their holiest day of worship?

Does God ask the Jews and the Christians to perform pilgrimage in Jerusalem or Rome?

Since the Quran was revealed in Arabic, it makes it easy for any Muslim to worship at any Mosque that is available when it is time to offer prayer (Salat). Muslims traveling from one country to another do not need to know the local languages but will understand the same language when it comes to the prayer because the prayer will be said in Arabic. All the five daily prayers are the same all over the world. That is the uniqueness and the beauty of Islam.

Do other religions have all these aforementioned proofs and evidence stated in their scriptures and act accordingly?

In conclusion, now that the truth has been said with the facts presented to you, you have the free will to make your choice as to what religion to follow.

May God guide us unto the right path (ameen).

Glo ssar y

Malaika - Means angels from the plural of Arabic (malak).

Jinn: an intelligent spirit of lower rank than the angels. Jinn are made of smokeless fire.

Jibrīl, also spelled Jabrā'īl, in Islām, the archangel who acts as intermediary between God and man and as bearer of revelation to the prophets, most notably, to Muḥammad. In biblical literature Gabriel is the counterpart to Jibrīl.

Isra and **Mi'raj**, also known as **Al Isra' wal Miraj**, is observed on the 27th day of the month of Rajab, the seventh month in the Islamic calendar. This event marks the night that Allah (God) took Muhammad (pbuh) on a journey from Mecca to Jerusalem and then to heaven and back to Mecca.

Makkah= Mecca

The Sidrat al-Muntahā (Arabic): is a Lote tree that marks the end of the seventh heaven, the boundary where no creation can pass.

Hijra: the flight of Muhammad from Mecca to Medina to escape Quraysh persecution 622 A.D. It is regarded as the beginning of the Muslim Era. 2. the Muslim Era itself. Expand. Also, Hegira, *Hijrah*.

SAW: Sallā Allāhu ʿalayhi wa- ala ālihi **wa-sallam**. It's an expression affixed with the mention of the Prophet Muhammad. It's basically a prayer for him and a way to express respect and gratitude towards him. Literally it means 'Allah sent prayer upon him and peace.' Popularly it's translated as 'May blessing and peace be upon him' or 'peace be upon him.'

Isa= Jesus Musa= Moses

Sulaiman= Solomon Idris= Enock Dawud= David

Iblis = Satan, Lucifer, Devil and Shaitan.

References

1 – The Holy Quran by Abdullah Yusuf Ali.

2 – Is Jesus a Christian or Muslim? 2nd edition, by Umar Sallau Al Hassan.

3 – The Quran: the Final Revelation to Mankind, by Conveying Islamic Message Society, Alexandra, Egypt.

4 – Sheik Yussuf Adepoju.

5 – http://islam.stackexchange.com/questions.

6 – Samuel Green www.answering.Islam.org/Green/union.htm.– Heroes and Hero Worship, by Thomas Carlyle. Article published in 1841.

7 – http://soulreadingzone.com/tag/covenant.with-god.

8 – Mallam Lukmon Adeyemo.

9 – Sheik Muhammad Awal.

10 – A Brief Illustrated Guide to Understanding Islam, Second Edition, by I. A. Ibrahim.

11 – Al Minhaj Al Muslim, Volume 1, by Abu Bakr Jabir

12 – Ustaz Jamiu Adegunwa.

13 – Late Sheik Ahmad Dida.

14 – The Holy Bible, King James Study Bible.

15 - The Holy Quran, by Mushaf Al- Madinah An-Nabawiyah.

www.ingramcontent.com/pod-product-compliance
Lightning Source LLC
Chambersburg PA
CBHW071002120626
46546CB00003B/892